STAY WITH ME

ME

DESTINED TO BE WITH YOU...

APARNA SHARMA

Copyright © Aparna Sharma
All Rights Reserved.

ISBN 978-1-63886-401-1

This book has been published with all efforts taken to make the material error-free after the consent of the author. However, the author and the publisher do not assume and hereby disclaim any liability to any party for any loss, damage, or disruption caused by errors or omissions, whether such errors or omissions result from negligence, accident, or any other cause.

While every effort has been made to avoid any mistake or omission, this publication is being sold on the condition and understanding that neither the author nor the publishers or printers would be liable in any manner to any person by reason of any mistake or omission in this publication or for any action taken or omitted to be taken or advice rendered or accepted on the basis of this work. For any defect in printing or binding the publishers will be liable only to replace the defective copy by another copy of this work then available.

I dedicate this book to someone who is close to my heart yet miles away from me.

Contents

Preface vii

Acknowledgements ix

Prologue xi

1. Transfer To A New School — 1
2. I'm Lost! — 4
3. The Coolest? The Worst! — 8
4. The Four Famous Guys Of School — 14
5. Sitting Arrangements — 18
6. First Kiss — 25
7. Accident Escape! — 30
8. Dona — 37
9. The Revenge — 41
10. The Novel Reading — 49
11. The Test — 54
12. Unexpected Shock! — 59
13. Girlfriend? — 65
14. He Became The Cold One Again — 72
15. Just Stranger Treatment — 77
16. Ava And I Became Close — 84
17. The Transfer — 91
18. The Fight — 96
19. Charles Riddle — 107
20. The Movie Night — 113
21. I Fell For Him — 124

Contents

22. Debate	131
23. Camping	138
24. I Like You	143
25. 4 Months Later...	147
The Birthday List Of Characters	151

Preface

The story is about a young girl pursuing her career and due to his father's job transfer, she ends up geting admitted in the top school of the respective city where she encounters four guys among which one was hard to get along with and she picked up fight with the school hunk which means, within 10 minutes of entering the school, she became the enemy of more than half of the girls in the campus.

After being blackmailed by him due to her certain things, she ends up being the fake girlfriend.

But gradually this feeling of hatred started changing. There were some other feelings yeilding in both the youngsters.
It was not just the feeling of friendship. It was love.

But it is said, realizing love is not that easy, and then confessing it is even harder.

How will they be realising it?
Whatever the turn this story takes, it'll be sweet

enough to melt your heart.

Acknowledgements

I would like to thank all the people who helped me all this while.

Thanks to:

My mom, dad, uncle, and aunt for their continuous support.

▷▷▷

- *Kinjel for making me love novels*
- *Meha for being the first one to read my novel*
- *Garvit and Mehul for secret support*
- *Sijal, Palak, Anushka, Anshu, Krish, Anant, Himani, and Manvi for encouragement.*
- *My youngest reader Yavi.*
- *My evertime supporter Jahnvi and Manjari.*

▷▷▷

Special thanks to my gems Prachi, Maithily, Kook Nochu, and my MangaToon readers.

▷▷▷

Also a big thanks to G. Chana Ma'am, Lucy Ma'am, and Uma Ma'am for teaching me and making me love literature.

▷▷▷

Prologue

There are many phases and secrets of Steven which Amelia is unknown about.

Will these secrets make her more closer to her or make them fall apart?

How will they fight these misunderstandings and trust issues for their love.

How will be their journey from enemies to lovers, from doubts to trust, from misunderstandings to understandings and lastly....
From NEVER to FOREVER.

1
Transfer to a New School

"Oh! what the hell! again a new school. Please dad not again." I screamed when I got to know that I was going to shift to a new school. This was the fifth time I was changing my school. So I denied changing the school. "Sweety you know the work of dad well. We can't do anything. My company keeps transferring me. You're a grown-up child, you must understand." pleaded my dad. Since I only had dad as my family so I finally agreed after understanding dad's situation.

The next day, the first day of school. well, I couldn't expect to make any close friends 'cause I knew that I might not be able to be with them for a long time. With this disappointment, I finally got dressed up to my new school, HEATHROW HIGH SCHOOL. My father gave me a forehead kiss and went to his workplace. I also headed to my new school.

I entered the school and just after walking few steps ahead I had only one thing in my mind, 'How can dad call this school the best school in this city.' Everyone there was busy with something stupid. A group of girls was doing the makeup of each other like they aren't here to study but to take part in a beauty contest. After walking a few more steps I found a group of boys showing their muscles to each other and asking every passerby if they looked or not. Well to me they were looking not less than stupids. Then a few steps ahead I saw another group who were practicing to propose to their crush. This was not just the end of stupidity. The more steps I'll take the more crackheads I would see.

While I was viewing this unbelievable scenario of a school, suddenly a football hit me on my head. My hair became a bit messy. I rubbed my head with my head and tried to set my hair. The four boys who were playing with that ball came to me. I was a bit angry but to avoid trouble I apologized to them instead of picking up a fight. "I'm sorry," I said. One of them picked the ball. And stepped aside without uttering a single word. They completely ignored my apology. So without wasting any single moment I stepped to head to the counter. Even before I could take a single step, a boy from those four stood in front of me and blocked my way.

"Excuse me, Mr. I've already apologized to you now what else you want?" I asked.

"Your apology had no sincerity," he said.

"What! And who are you to comment on my words?"

"It doesn't matter who I am. Apologize to me sincerely for your mistake."

"What the hell you are. According to what happened right now, it must be you who should say sorry but I apologized to show my dignity. Instead of being thankful for forgiving you and taking the initiative of apologizing, you are blaming me and asking for a sincere apology."

"So now you even dared to blame me. Listen to me carefully girl. It was you who came in my way of goal, so it's completely your fault."

"Are you completely a crackhead. You're blaming me. Instead of playing in football ground, you were playing in walking area and then telling me that I came in way of your goal."

"It's my choice I'll play wherever I want to."

"Then this is also my choice, I will walk wherever I want to. Now step aside."

Still he wasn't stepping aside. So, kicked hard on his leg. He stepped aside just within a second. I headed towards the counter. But in between our fight I at least realised that he wasn't someone to get rid off easily. 'cause when we were fighting, everyone left their work and gathered around us. And the expressions were telling that I've surely offended someone who his hardest to deal with in this campus.

Well, I had no time to think about this problem anymore as my class was about to begin in ten minutes and I still didn't collect my ID Card from the counter. I rushed to the counter.

"Excuse me, I'm a new student in the school and want my ID Card."

"Hello! Welcome to our school. Your name and age please."

"Amelia Somerson, 16 yrs."

"Alright, here is your Id Card, your class room number is 19."

"Okay, Thank You."

"Your welcome."

2
I'm Lost!

After getting my Id Card, I rushed to my classroom. I began searching for room number 19. I went upstairs and then downstairs, and repeated again and again, but I wasn't able to find my classroom. After a few moments, I stopped and looked here and there. I was fully exhausted after realizing that I again reached the place where I started.

"What the heck! I'm again at the starting." I thought of asking someone but no one was there, even the counterperson was gone somewhere. I was scolding myself that how can I be so stupid that I'm even lost in a school. I was looking for someone to help me out. Suddenly, I saw a guy coming towards me. I was about to ask him but I stopped as soon as I realized that he was one of those three friends of that crackhead.

I found it better to look for the way of class myself than to ask him. I turned around and start walking. But he recognized me and shouted from there, "Hey, Ms. Kicking Girl!" I stopped and turned around.

He came and stood in front of me.

"So I wasn't mistaken. You're really Ms. Kicking Girl."

"Firstly, he deserved that kick, and secondly, stop calling me kicking girl. It sucks."

He started laughing and then said, "Alright, I was just having some fun. I won't call you that again. Well, your confidence in front of him was awesome. It was really something worth praising to."

"Hey, aren't you his friend?"

"Of course, I am. In fact, We're best friends."

"Then why are you praising me. Is this what you called friendship."

"Hey, firstly, all three of us know that you were right, so why would we take his side. Secondly, it was the first time that girl dared to talk to him like that and even hit him, so why won't we laugh and enjoy that moment. That's what real friendship is. You would also have many friends with who you'll be like this. Don't you?"

I was speechless to that question, 'cause I never had such friends. I only had one friend in my middle school but with her too I gradually lost contact because of the transfer of both of our fathers to different places.

While I was grieving my loneliness, he interrupted, "Leave it. Well, are you wandering here?"

"You think to want to wander here? It's just that I.. I..."

"Hey, don't say me that.... you're lost."

My silence to his assumption already proved his assumption right.

"You really are lost", then he started laughing.

"Hey, stop laughing. Isn't normal for a person to get lost at the new place."

"Is it? I don't think so. Especially when it's just a school."

"Alright, stop laughing, if you can help then please do, or else I'll look for someone else."

"You think I'm so mean that I'll not help out a 'lost student in school', tell me your class number."

"It's 19"

"No way! you're not kidding me right."

"What's there to joke about in the classroom."

"No, I mean that's great that you're in Room number 19"

"Why? What's so special in this?"

"Now, our class will have daily entertainment."

"Why?"

"Use, that brain of yours and think about it."

I thought about it a little, but the aura around me proved that it'll really be a big issue. I thought about his words, I had already assumed what he was trying to tell me. I looked at him with a tense expression and said, "Hey, don't say that I'm in class the same as you and that crackhead."

"That's right. Welcome, our new classmate."

"No that can't be. I can't be in the same class as that of him."

"But, babes that's what the truth is. Now, you can't change the decision of the school. What you can do is to pray that he doesn't bring you any problem. Now lemme take you to your new classroom. Let's go."

I followed him on the way to the classroom. I was really thinking of myself as the most unlucky girl. I never thought that the person whom I wanted to avoid would be my classmate.

While I was following him, I was continuously thinking that how to deal with a crackhead. The friend of that guy realized my tension and said, "Don't worry, Steven is not that bad. He's just a bit cold."

"So, the name of that crackhead is Steven."

"Yea, his name is Steven, and I'm Eden. Nice to meet you. What's you're name."

"Myself Amelia Somerson"

"Nice name." he complimented.

Meanwhile, we reached the class. I sighed with relief as Steven wasn't there in meantime. So, I was at ease for few moments.

3
The Coolest? The Worst!

I looked here and there to find an empty seat. I found an empty seat and sit over there. I looked at the time table "Great! finally something good. The first lecture is of calculus." I don't know why many people hate this subject but I like this subject.

So before the class start and the teacher arrive, I took out my book and notebook and started solving my first unit myself. Well don't think of me as a studious person, 'cause I was solving questions 'cause I wasn't getting any meaningful excuse to avoid Steven when he'll enter the class.

The bell of the first lecture rang. Those four boys entered the class. I was trying to ignore them completely. But the environment of the class didn't let me do that. Every girl was staring at them so delightfully like there is no one alive in the world except for them. Suddenly, Steven looked at me. I was scared if he'll really bring death to me today. But the outcome was different. He moved his face in another direction, showing me complete ignorance. I was a relief for once that he won't revenge on me, but the another second Eden waved his hand to me and said, "Hey, Ms. Kicking Girl!

I'm back."

I got stuck in the position I was as if that if I'll move, I'll be beheaded. After hearing this, Steven stopped on his way to his seat and looked at me with his icy cold eyes for a moment, and then headed towards the seat.

After few moments, our calculus teacher, Mr. Watson entered the class.

"Morning students. So welcome to the new session. This is your first day of high school. From today onwards only, we need to work hard on our subjects so that we won't have any problem. So let's start with the first chapter of Calculus. Open your books and notebooks all of you."

Everyone took out the notebook and was ready for the first chapter. The teacher was about to start the chapter when suddenly a girl came at the door and asked in a loud voice, "Sir, may I get in?"

Mr. Watson looked at the door and said, "Oh! as expected, it's you, Ms. Collins."

"Good Morning Sir, Sorry to be late."

"Ava, you're not in middle school now, you're in high school. Still so irresponsible."

"I'm so sorry sir, I promise to be on time from tomorrow."

"This is more than the 100th time you're promising me. When can you fulfill it."

"Sir, leave the past. Today I'm assuring you that I'll be on time from tomorrow."

"I don't know how to tackle you. Well, sit down first and take out a notebook for the first lecture."

"Alright, sir. Thank you."

She came inside the class and searched for an empty seat, the only empty seat left was a seat beside me. So she came to me and asked if she can sit with me. She was quite frank and her nature was nice so I agreed.

Then I sincerely attended the class. After the class, there was a short break of five minutes. We put our notebooks inside. Ava turned to me and said, "Hello! It seems that you're a new student."

"Yea!" I replied.

"Well myself Ava Collins. And you?"

"I'm Amelia Somerson."

"Nice to meet you", we said together.

She had a very different aura. Her nature was really good and she seemed to be carefree. This really attracted me a lot. Then she asked me to be her friend. I agreed. And finally, I made my first friend in that school. In this way, we became friends and after that, we attended every class with full concentration. Then there was recess time. I hated this period of time a lot because everyone ate with their friends but I never made friends so I used to eat alone and envied others.

Hence, as usual, I started eating my lunch alone.

Ava came with one of her friends and said, "Hey, Amelia, why didn't you wait for me. I just went to take my friend with me to have lunch with us but you started eating."

"Oh, I'm sorry. I thought that you had your own plans."

"Oh, Sweety. What are you saying? We're friends now. And from now on, we'll have lunch together."

I wasn't able to explain how much I was happy, 'cause they didn't know that I never had a close friend except for my Middle School friend. Well, after that we started eating lunch. Ava introduced her friend to me.

"Amelia, she's Mia. Mia, she's...."

Mia interrupted in between. "She's Amelia Somerson. The kicking girl! Right!"

I asked in a shocking way, "How can this news be everywhere."

Mia replied, "Dude! you tried to challenge the limit of the coolest guy and hunk of the school and you're asking how is this news everywhere. C'mon girl, he's a crush of more than half of the girls in the school."

Ava didn't understand anything. So she said, "Hey, the way in which you both are talking I'm sure that you're about Steven. But what exactly happened."

Mia replied, "Ava you must have come earlier today 'cause you missed the best and once in a lifetime scene."

"Why? What happened."

"Today, in the morning, 15 minutes before the school started, she picked up a fight with Steven and she even kicked him on his leg to make him step aside and that too in front of whole campus."

Ava was sort of in a state of shock. "My goodness, Amelia, you really pick up a fight with Steven?"

I replied full of my confidence, "Well, it wasn't me who picked up a fight with him. It was he himself. His ball hit me, then I showed my dignity and apologised to him. But he said that I wasn't sincere enough in my apology. Then I fought for my justice."

"Woah! Amelia, I thought that you were a silent girl who won't be able to fight back. But it's totally the opposite. You're the first person who offended Steven. I'm really your fan now. but you might have got many enemies on your first day especially those lovesick girls as you've offended their highness. For everyone in the school, he's the coolest guy."

I replied, "The Coolest? The Worst! Let me tell you, I'm neither afraid of Steven nor his fangirls. I don't give a damn about him. He's just a fucking idiot in front of me...."

Ava tried to stop me, "Amelia I think you must stop or else you'll be in trouble."

I replied with full enthusiasm," Hey, Ava, don't be afraid of him. He's just a freaking jerk, a fucking idiot. Nothing else. He doesn't even have the courage to stand in front of me. What can he do to me....."

I was about to continue my words but Ava and Mia had very tensed expressions and they told me to stop talking and look back.

I looked back. And to my horror, Steven was in front of me. I was thinking if he had listened to everything I said about him while standing behind me. I was thinking about what he's gonna do to me.

I tried to smile in front of him and said, "Hi Mr. Steven, I think you've not heard even a bit right!"

"What if I say that I've heard every single bit of it."

"You heard it? Then, let's forget it okay. Why pick up the fight again."

"But as what I heard, I'm even not courageous enough to stand in front of you."

"haha.... that was... just a joke. Please don't take it to the heart."

"I can't understand. How can you be so shameless that you were just talking behind anyone's back. Haven't your mother taught you anything"

This was too much for me to tolerate. I was silent in front of him for the sake of my father. But then, he involved my mother, who died fours years ago when I was twelve years old.

So, without thinking for a single second, I shouted at him, "Who the fuck you're to tell me how should I behave and what should I talk about. Remember one thing carefully that don't ever bring my mother in our arguments. It's really good that I just kicked you at your leg, didn't slapped you or else it would have been more embarrased for you. I'm tolerating you just for the sake of my father. Or else I sear that I would have beaten you up. And if you think that I can't fight that let me tell you that I'm a black belt in Karate. So you must be thankful for my mercy on you. Now get out of my way."

After speaking too much, I pushed him away and went to the classroom for my next class.

4
The four famous guys of School

After saying so much to him I got a sudden feeling of courage. I was then confident that I can face him fearlessly. Though now I was in such a situation that I couldn't decide what to do after I would be in front of him again. What if he would be forceful in another meeting? What if he tried to harm me? So many questions were there in my mind. But the only thing I could do at that time was to be calm and go with the flow. So I quietly came at my seat and sat there.

The recess was over. Ava and Mia also came to the class. Ava came and sat. She was continuously looking at me. I finally asked her, "What happened? Since you came, you're continuously looking at my face. Is there something on my face?"

"No no, it's just that I'm impressed by your bravery. The way you talked to him was awesome. How were even able to do that."

"Actually I might not have done that if he had not included my mother. But he did. So, I needed to give an answer. Hence, I finally shouted at him. And it was his fault anyway. But, now I don't know what to do. What if he'll try to harm me?"

"Oh, c'mon girl. He cannot do anything to you if his best friends deny him to do so."

"And why you think that they'll try to protect me?"

"Dude you think too much. Of course, they don't interfere in others' matters but we'll make sure that Steven doesn't revenge on you."

"How?"

"Oh, my silly girl. Lemme tell you everything about them from the very start. So here it goes.....

Steven is also known as the school hunk. Nearly every girl falls for him because of his good looks. But he has never given attention to a single girl. So, this quality of his makes him the coolest guy in the school. Steven is rarely seen without his best friends. He has three best friends. Rason, Eden, and Zeo.

Rason is also very cool. He rarely talks to girls. And to be honest, for me, he's the most fucking guy ever. 'Cause previously we used to share the same seat and this guy is so boring that he never talked anything. Sometimes I wonder, how can someone be so quiet. What god made his mouth for? Just for eating? Anyways, let's come to another one.

Zoe Oliver is the only person who's a bit normal. He's mostly nice to everyone, except for his enemies. He deals with them in the worst way. He would not let any of his enemies harm his beloved girl, our friend, and his girlfriend, Mia. Next one...

Eden Froster is the frankest guy in these four. He is sometimes so childish that when he'll not get anything to do, he'll just start counting and making a list of the people who got beaten by these four. Don't be shocked after hearing this. Actually, many people keep challenging them different things to look cool but end up being beaten up by them. Well, though he's a bit childish that doesn't mean that he's easygoing. Once a guy tried to force Janice to kiss, so he beat him up so badly that he was in a coma for nearly 5 months."

"Who is Janice?"

"Oh, yea! I forgot to tell you about her before. actually, I, Janice, and Mia have always been together. We three are best friends. But right now she's on an educational trip. I'll make you meet her after she comes back."

"Oh! Alright. But why Eden helped her?"

"Things might have been different if there was someone else. But Janice is the one whom he loves. So he won't let her hurt in any way."

"My god! seems that they aren't easy to be dealt with at all. They all seem to be very furious."

"Or else why you think that the news that you argued with him and hit him would have flown so fast, even faster than celebrity rumors."

"So, will he revenge on me too?"

"Maybe he'll try to, but don't worry I don't think that he'll harm you. 'Cause he doesn't know how to tackle a girl."

"Really!"

"Of course! Can't you guess it yourself? He didn't know what to do that's why you were escaped by him. 'Cause he always has dealt with the boys and that too with fights. "

"Oh! then it's fine. But then too I think I must avoid him as much as I can."

"But... I don't think you can do it 'cause Mia is the girlfriend of Zeo and Eden likes Janice and I have lunch with her and Janice only so we have our lunch with those four. And now you're also my friend so you'll also accompany me, won't you?"

She thought of me as her close friend, so of course, I couldn't deny it. Hence, I agreed.

From the next day, I needed to have lunch with those Idiots, especially that crackhead so that only meant that I would only have a single day of a peaceful lunch and that would be Sunday. I was pitying myself for having such luck. It was just my first day and such horrible things happened that I've never encountered in my life before. Though I never had any close friends except for Jane then too at least my life was peaceful enough that I didn't argue with anyone or hit anyone on the first day of school.

He was no less than a curse for me. I would rather live with my enemies than to be his classmate. But, I had no other option so I encouraged myself 'cause I was trying to calm down just so that I won't cause any trouble to my father, but he wasn't the type of person who could be dealt with calmness so I promised myself that no matter what I won't let him bully me.

Meanwhile I was thinking all these stuffs, I didn't realise that the last lecture was over and I needed to go home. I packed up my bag and rushed to home.

Finally, I reached home and it was then when I was totally relieved

5
Sitting Arrangements

———•♡•———

The next day, I was all set to go the school that too without any worry 'cause I knew my potential. So without any delay, I rushed to the school. I went and decided to sit on the first bench as I was early in the class and no one was there to occupy that seat and I don't think that anyone in that class would do that, 'cause everyone there craved for the last bench.

Hence, I put my bag and went out of class to roam around until Ava arrives. The moment I stepped out of the class, Ava came running and panting. I stopped her and asked her what happened.

She replied, "Amelia! I'm very happy. Yippeee!"

"But what happened?"

"Janice is coming today. It's been a long time since I last saw her. Finally, she's back. You know everyone in the school is discussing her return."

"Why? She isn't a celebrity."

"But she's no less than a celebrity. You know what if Steven is said to be the most handsome guy in this campus, then Janice is the most beautiful girl. Many students have even try to ship them with each other but they cleared it in front of all that they think of each other as brother and sister. That's why Eden has a chance to woo her."

"Wow! it seems she's really popular here."

"Of course she is. But... I think that since yesterday, you're the most popular here."

"C'mon Ava, don't bring that topic again. I've already decided to let it go."

"Alright, alright. I won't talk about this again."

While we were talking, Mia came and said, "Come fast. She's back. She has arrived at the school."

Ava said with excitement, "Wow! that's great. Let's go. Amelia, you also come with us."

She held my hand took me with her. We went to the school reception where she was. As I reached, I saw the girl's back and those four were in from of her and talking about her trip. Well, his face wasn't bothering me anymore because I don't keep anything for too long. Mia called Janice and she turned back.

I was all shocked to see that it was Jane, which means that Jane was Janice.

Ava ran to her and hugged her. And she suddenly looked at me and s was all surprised to see me. She loosens the hug with Mia and was continuously looking at me with tears of happiness in her eyes. I was also looking at her in the same way.

I said in a very light voice, "Jane!"

"Amelia, you... I thought I would never see you again"

"Me too..."

We ran towards each other and hugged each other. Both were crying as well as smiling.

None of them was understanding what was going on there.

Eden said, "You know each other?"

Jane answered, "She is my best friend. We were together in the first year of middle school. After that, I was transferred here and she was transferred to another place. At that time, my father's sim was lost so he bought a new one. And I lost contact with her. It's been two years since we talked and met."

Eden turned to me and said, "That means, Amelia you knew that she studied here. That's why you came to study here."

I replied, "I even didn't know where she lived these two years, how can I Know her school. Even I didn't know that she has changed her name from Jane to Janice."

Janice cleared herself that her real name is Janice only but everyone called her Jane there so that's why I remember her name as Jane.

After these all talks, we went to class. Jane sat with me and Mia and then Eden and Steven also sat on the first bench in the row next to us. Rason and Zeo and sat just behind them.

Eden tried to talk to Jane. But I stopped him, "Hey Eden. Can you please gimme some time to talk to her? It's been a long time since we talked."

Steven replied on behalf of him, "So just take her home today and talk as long as you want to."

I replied in a rude way, "I think you must mind your own business. That doesn't concern you. Don't jump between others' talk."

"Eden is my friend. Of course, I can. Why you have a problem with that."

"Mr. Steven, can you not indulge in this?"

"You wish."

"You crackhead, what's your problem. Cant, you talk in a polite manner."

"Why should I talk to an impolite girl in a polite manner?"

"You... it's really a waste of time to argue with you 'cause you can never be nice to me."

"You really expect me to be nice to you, the one kicked me in front of the whole school."

Jane was hearing all this. She stopped us and said, "Wait, a kick to Steven?"

Eden explained everything to Jane and she was continuously laughing after hearing all this. While I was still thinking to change the environment, the teacher entered the class. I was really thankful to god at that time.

It was a History lecture. The teacher of History was also our class teacher.

He was Mr. Torvald. He was a strict teacher too.

He came in class, we greeted him morning and sat on our seats quietly. He announced, "Students. I want my class to be totally disciplined so for this I'll change your seats according to what I think is the best for you. From now on, a girl and a boy will sit on each seat. Right now you're sitting in rows. One row is full of boys and the other is full of girls. Now y'all need to exchange the seats with any one student on the bench next to you. Let's start with the first bench. Eden, you exchange your seat with Amelia, Amelia you go to Steven."

I screamed with horror, "What! Sir no... please. Cant, I sit somewhere else."

"I won't hear anything, Sit where I'm telling you too."

Steven stood up and said, "Sir, cant you let me sit alone. I don't wanna sit with this girl."

The teacher said in a scolding way, "What's the problem with you two? Am I going to make sitting arrangements according to you? Just say as I do. Eden, come here and

Amelia, go there."

We had no other option. I needed to sit with him from that day. He was the most horrible bench mate I got. I was doubting my luck so much that I was even thinking to check my Yin Yang. But I don't think that we two were the only people who were feeling disgusted by this.

The teacher came to the second seat and said, "Ava and Zeo, exchange your seats. Zeo you come to Mia and Ava you go to Rason."

Zeo and Mia were happy but Ava and Rason were not willing to sit with each other.

Ava said to sir, "Sir, please. I can't sit with this guy again?"

Rason added, "Sir, even I can't sit with her."

Sir said with a furious voice, "What's wrong with you people. Just a moment before, Steven and Amelia were making a fuss, and now you two. Just sit silently."

Ava silently went to his seat, but the only thinking of one thing, 'God! how can you make me bear him once again? He's such a boring guy.'

Rason was also very disgusted and was thinking, 'God, how can you make me sit with this girl again. She speaks too much that I'll get a headache within an hour.'

But, like me and the crackhead, they were also forced to do so.

Within five minutes, Mr. Torvald was done with sitting arrangements. Then he started the class.

We silently studied.

After the lecture was over, we had five minutes break. But this break was useless for me because I was sitting with Steven.

After the teacher went away, Steven said, "Hey, if you're sitting with me then you better not test my patience and stay quiet."

"And you think I would listen to you?"

"Then try not listening to me."

"Mr. Steven Young! don't you think that you think too highly of yourself? Do you think that I will listen to you? How can you expect it from me? I'm not one of those lovesick girls who are totally blind. Let me tell you, a girl like me will never listen to you."

"Are you trying to play hard to get?"

"What! Mr. Crackhead, can you please not think too highly of yourself? You know what, I will never like a guy like you at least in my this life, then how can you expect me to play hard to get in front of you?"

"I don't understand how girls like you exist..."

"And I don't understand how guys like you exist... who think so highly of themselves"

"I think so highly of myself because that's what I really am. But people like you get jealous of my fame."

"Dude, there are 7 billion people in the world and ill get jealous of you, the one who is just nothing to me."

"You're continuously offending me. You know that you can be in trouble by doing this?"

"Who do you think you are that you're capable of making me miserable."

"Even if I don't do anything, but what if the girls in this school know about this. If they got to know that you're wooing me, they'll make your life hell. And in this, I won't need to anything. I'll just watch the show. The title of the show GIRLS FIGHTING WITH EACH OTHER FOR A SCHOOL HUNK"

I made the worst expressions I could ever make after listening to his nonsense. I didn't give a damn to those things and directly, "Alright, do whatever you want. I knew that you aren't capable of holding a grudge against me, but I never thought that you would be so helpless that you'll need those lovesick girls to take revenge on your behalf."

"Girl, you'll regret whatever you said to me today."

"Then we'll see when I will really do regret it."

I think this fight would have gone longer if the teacher wouldn't have arrived on time. Thankfully, she arrived on time.

6

First Kiss

We somehow tried to be quiet till the last period. The last period was of Sports. I was finally relieved that now I didn't need to tolerate that guy again.

With happiness on my face, I went to the playground with Jane, Ava, and Mia.

We decided to play Basketball. And the guys went to play Football.

while we were playing, I suddenly tripped and fell down. When I tried to stand up again, I wasn't able to and then I realized that I sprained my ankle. Now I didn't know what to to do. Suddenly a girl shouted in the playground, "Amelia fell down and sprained her leg."

All the girls stopped there and came to me. Even the boys too stopped playing and came to me.

The whole class gathered around me. Jane said to those people, "You're just looking at the injured girl, cant you help her."

Suddenly, Steven appeared from the crowd. He stepped towards and bent in front of me. I thought he's gonna lecture me again. But he instead took out his jacket and put it on me and held me up in his arms.

This was surprising. everyone was looking at us and this was kinda embarrassing. And also he mustn't have held me in his arms at least because for other people it was like a prince saving his princess, but for me, it was like a devil taking his prey to dine on it.

I shouted in embarrassment, fear, anger, "Hey, put me down. I can walk by myself."

But he totally ignored my words. I was trying to make myself free from his arms hold, but I wasn't able to 'cause he held me tightly. Somewhere I was feeling a bit comfortable but... I couldn't expect anything good from him because whatever happened between us till that time, according to that he could never help me.

Meanwhile, I was thinking this all, he took me to the infirmary and made me sit down on a chair. Then he said, "Don't move from here, or else I'll make sure that your both legs get broken."

"What the hell you are. You're even threatening at the time of help. How can a 17-year-old guy be so bossy. Just leave me in my own way. I'll help myself out."

He took out a spray from the cupboard and came to me and held my leg which was injured. Meanwhile, I was still shouting at him. He was so frustrated by my talk that he finally said, "If you don't shut your mouth now, then I'll do something that won't like at all."

"Mr. Crackhead, you can never harm me. You don't have that courage. And even if you do, I'll never let myself be weak in front of you."

Well, say I was trying to act rude or was overwhelmed by myself, I wasn't stopping even after he threatened me. I was continuously lecturing him and speaking ill about him.

He again said, "So you really won't stop."

"No, I won't stop even if you kill me. I swear even if I'll die, I'll become a ghost and will scare you every night. Listen to me, I'm not afraid of you. I'm really.........."

Before I could complete my words, he suddenly put his hand around my neck, the other in my waist, and kissed me. I was totally stunned. I didn't know what to do. It was my first kiss and I couldn't believe that my first kiss was with someone whom I hated.

At first, I wasn't even able to think what I must do, but after few seconds, I got a conscience and pushed him and then slapped him hard and said, "You Jerk! How can you be so shameless? You dared to kiss me. This is too much!"

I snatched the spray from his hand and started spraying on my leg by myself.

He tried to take it and said, "Lemme do it."

"No need, if you really wanna help me then do not ever appear in front of me again."

"Why are you so stubborn. It was just a kiss. Why making it such a big issue."

"Just a kiss! Alright, it's me who is making it such a big issue. Are you happy now?"

Before he could say anything else, I had already applied the spray on my sprain and tried to stand up. He again tried to help me by giving me support by his hand, but I was so disgusted by his act that I pushed his hand and said, "I already said that I'll do it myself."

He indicated me to let him help me by saying, "Do you want that everyone gets to know about our kiss? You don't want, right? Then obey me."

He left me with no choice. I couldn't let my father know about this. So, I let him help me. And I wasn't angry at him for his help. It's just that he even helped by threatening me.

He held me in his arms and took me to the class and made me sit on my seat and went to the playground again. Of course, I couldn't expect him to stay with me to take care of me.

After he went away, I was still thinking about my first kiss. I expected my first kiss to be romantic but it was rather the worst. What a perfect irony. While I was lost in my thoughts, Mia entered. She came to me and said, "Oh my, Amelia. Are you alright?"

"Yea! I am."

"That's great! I'll stay with you till this period gets over. Oh! By the way, you know you're at the top search on the school website of the students."

"Students even have their website?"

"Of course, they have. And you're the most popular search just in 15 minutes after you went to the infirmary."

"Why is it so?"

"A student in our class clicked the picture of Steven holding you in arms. And within 5 minutes this picture became so viral that after that within 10 minutes you became the most searched student of this month and that too just within 10 minutes."

"Was this incident such a big thing that everyone is searching about me?"

"It wasn't but, it became the one. Actually, you're the first girl whom Steven has ever touched. You're the first person whom he has held in his arms. You're the first girl who has ever dared to argue with him and that too numerous times. You're the first with whom he sits. You're the first girl to hit him. You're the reason to make many things first time in his life."

'That means that I'm his first kiss too...' I thought.

I never knew that he has never even touched a girl. By then I was having a doubt which asked to Mia even without thinking. I said, "Mia, then, is he a gay or a straight guy?"

Mia laughed hard and then said, "He's a straight guy. Don't worry. hahaha"

After hearing her response, I was embarrassed about my question.

Well, by the time, the school got over.

Mia gave me a ride to my home as my ankle was still not cured. I reached home and I swear I didn't sleep that night 'cause whenever I would try to sleep, that crackhead and his kiss would appear in my mind.

7
Accident Escape!

The next day I woke up, not with the sound of an alarm clock, but because of a call.

I looked at my phone. It was Steven's call. I really didn't want to pick up but I couldn't go back on my words. Hence, I picked up my phone.

"Good morning!" he said.

"Why you called me in such early hours?"

"Do you have a car?"

"What?"

"Do you have a car?"

"Oh I heard it but why you want my car?"

"Come and fetch me."

"What?"

"Do you have any hearing problems?"

"No."

"Then why are you not able to hear anything. Can't you respond like a normal person?"

"Dude! you wanna make my response normal? Do you think that the way 'you called me in such early hours and then asked me to come and fetch you' is normal?"

"Don't forget what you said yesterday. You'll do anything to repay me."

"But I never said to do such lousy things."

"That doesn't matter. And also listen, from now onwards you're my PA."

"Say that again!"

"See, I told you that you've got a hearing problem."

"You clearly know the meaning of my words. I'm giving you a chance to change your words."

"What if I don't?"

"I said to take back your words or else..."

"Or else."

"Or else I... I'll do as you say."

"Good girl."

"Hey, can't you have some mercy on me?"

"You wish. I'm hanging up. Come fast."

"Hey, wait, I..."

Before I could say anything else, he hung up.

I stepped outta bed and headed to the bathroom when I got a notification. I checked my notification and got to know that it was from that crackhead. I opened the message. In the message, the following words were written:

To Amelia Somerson,

You've just 45 minutes. Your time starts now.

-Steven Young

"Aahhhh! What the heck this guy is.", I shouted in anger. And then rushed to get ready.

I think it was the first time in my life that I got ready within 10 minutes. If my father wasn't on a business then he might have thought that I've got a fever or a head injury.

Then I rushed to the car and after sitting in the car, I realized that I don't know his address.

I called him. He picked up and said, "Say."

"Where do you live?"

"I'm sending you the address."

He hung up.

Within few seconds, he sent the address. I checked his address and realized that he lives far away from me. That would take me nearly 45 minutes. And I had... (looked at the watch,) "Just 25 minutes! Has he gone totally, crazy!", I shouted and then rushed to the address he sent.

After 45 minutes, I reached there.

He was standing at the gate of his house. And I swear that house was so big and luxurious that my next few generations can stay there collectively.

While I was continuing to enjoy the view of the house, that idiot flicked my hair. I said, "What're you doing?"

"Stop looking here and there and open the gate for me."

"Can't you open it yourself?"

He said nothing but turned his face.

I swear I hadn't encountered such an arrogant guy before.

But I wasn't in any mood to argue in the early morning so I just quietly opened the door and let him sit.

Right after he sitting in the car, he said, "You're late by 25 minutes."

"What else you expect? 10 minutes of getting ready, then, 45 minutes of reaching here. In total, 55 minutes, and you expect me to be here in 30 minutes. So inhumane."

He gave a cunning smile and then said, "Let's go."

I drove the car as fast as I could to take my revenge.

Well, I thought that he'll yell at me for driving so fast, but... he was... sacred.

He grabbed the sides of his seat and held it firmly. Then he said, "Hey, You wanna kill me today! Slow down."

"What if I don't?"

"You... just slow down. Or else, you're gonna regret it later."

"We'll see about it later."

"How can you be so stubborn, girl. You know it's the highest speed of this car."

"Don' worry. I'm experienced."

"Put your experience aside. The next road is a very busy road. You really gonna send me to heaven today."

"Oh My... how can you expect your place in heaven? I doubt even if hell will be having a place for you or not."

"Hey, how can you joke around like this? I'm serious."

"I'm also serious. Forget about heaven, you won't even be accepted in hell."

"Hey, can you stop this heaven, hell, and purgatory? Just slow down."

I wasn't listening to him at all. I was just busy teasing him and saying all ill words for him. For a second I looked at him, but at the very same time, a truck came from nowhere towards us.

He screamed, "Hey! Watch out!" and then moved the steering wheel towards the other direction.

I applied the brake. We were really about to bump into that truck if not for him helping me.

I was all shocked. We both were sitting in a still position for nearly 5 minutes.

Then I realized that I overestimated my driving skills. Of course, I couldn't drive at a fast speed on a busy road.

After taking and releasing a deep breath, he said, "Who gave you the driving license?"

"I'm sorry. This time, it was my fault. I must not have driven at such high speed. I... I was trying to tease you."

"Tease me! Is this a way you tease someone by risking that person's life? Leave about that person. You can at least care about your life. Are you a total idiot!"

"Hey, can you stop scolding me now? I've already accepted that I'm wrong."

"If apologies work, why do we need police?"

"But we're saved."

"We're saved 'cause I concentrated on the road ahead."

"Alright! why make a fuss about this? It's already over."

"Oh, so you want me to praise you!"

"Okay! I'm sorry. It was my fault. I'll drive carefully now. Check if your seatbelt is fastened. I'm starting the car."

"Wait! First, get outta the car."

"Why?"

"Just do as I said. I'm already pissed off!"

It was my fault anyway. So I did as he said.

Both of us got out of the car.

He said, "Listen carefully. I love my life a lot. And I'm not gonna sacrifice it because of such stupidity of yours. So, I'll drive the car."

"But I know how to drive. I already explained why I drove so fast."

"Then too I can't take the risk. Who knows, if next time you'll make this car jump from the bridge to the river."

I already understood that I couldn't fight with him. Hence, I decided to let him drive.

He drove the car.

Soon we reached the school. But despite getting up so early, I reached the school late from the usual timing I reached there.

We went to the class just 2 minutes before the class starts.

We sat on our bench, which was the worst seat I got 'cause it was with this crackhead.

Rason and Ava were sitting behind us.

Rason asked, "Why are you two late today? Have you got sickness like that of Ava?"

Ava said in anger, "Hey! Mind your words. Whether I get here early or late, what's to do with you? Brown noser."

"You even have got guts to call me brown noser, you... loquacious!"

She kicked Rason with his leg.

"Ouch! It hurts, are you trying to make me paralyzed." said rason rubbing his leg.

"Of course not, but I really wish to," said Ava.

I knew that if I wouldn't try to stop them, their fight will be never-ending.

Hence, I said, "Alright Alright! Can you please over this fight?"

They finally stopped.

Then Ava turned to me and said, "Well, why were you late."

That was the first time that even I thought that she speaks a lot.

I was planning to give a simple excuse like I woke up late. But that crackhead spilled out the beans.

He said, "A person was trying to overestimate her driving skills and nearly brought herself and the guy beside him to the death. Thank god that the guy handled the steering at the right time."

Ava said, "Don't tell me that these people are you two."

Steven said, "Who else."

"So, it's really you too. Hahaha..." laughed Ava.

I was really feeling very much embarrassed that I didn't know what to do.

I couldn't stop her laughing 'cause I knew it was my fault.

Rason got irritated by her laughter and said.

"Can you stop laughing?"

"Why?"

" 'Cause, it sucks."

"What's your problem? Why you meddle around my business."

"I won't. As long as it doesn't disturb me."

Their fights again started.

Eden looked at them and asked us, "What's going on with them."

I was going to give a simple answer when Steven said, "Nothing, just two people are flirting with each other."

Eden said with a weird expressions, "In this way?"

Both, Ava and Rason realized what Steven said and both of them shouted and said the same words , "Who is flirting with this kind of person."

Then looked at each other and then turned theirfaces in opposite directions.

I was relieved.

8
Dona

The next day, I went to school. I was all determined not to forgive that person for whatever he did. I would have totally ignored him but the major problem was that we shared the same desk, so I couldn't totally get rid of him. Well, the only thing I could do was to try to avoid him.

I reached the school. As I entered the class, I was stopped by a girl. She put her hand between the entranceway and after stopping me, she said, "Oh! So you're Amelia Somerson. The girl who is wooing Steven."

"Excuse me, I think you're mistaken. I'm not wooing him. I have no intention to be with him. Now please step aside. I need to get inside."

"How can you be so shameless. Everyone here knows that you're targeting him. Still, you're denying it."

"I was thinking to talk to you with respect, but don't deserve it."

"Who do you think you are? You are even lying that you didn't woo him. Just stop pestering Steven from now onwards or else the outcome will be the worst."

Steven was already being too much and now that girl too started irritating me. In anger, I said, "Yes! I'm pestering him. I'm wooing him. So what? What can you do?"

"You bitch you even dared to say it in such a way." She tried to slap me.

I held her hand before she could slap me and twisted her hand.

She screamed, "Ouch! It hurts, leave me."

"You better behave from next time. And next time before slapping or hitting me, keep in mind that I'm a black belt in karate. Though I usually never fight. But if a fucking bitch like you dared to the same thing again then don't expect me to go easy on you. I won't. And yes, whatever my relation is with Steven, it must not concern you. Now just fuck off!"

I let her go. I was really bursting with anger. Wherever I would go, I would hear the same gossips everywhere. I was so damn done with this that I finally lost my temper and twisted her hand.

I never expected that I would have a first meeting even worse than that of Steven. Well, she deserved it.

Later from the other people, I got to know that she's Dona Maxwell, sister of Rason. Well, it didn't concern me anymore, 'cause I knew it well that from next time, she'll only use her tongue instead of hands or other physical power.

I took the seat and started studying. After few minutes, Steven entered the class. It was the first time that he came alone, without his whole group. He came to me and took out his phone. Then he said, "Do me a favour."

"What do you want?"

"I....I.... wanna take a selfie with you."

I was totally surprised. I wasn't able to understand that what's wrong with that crackhead. Every student in the class was watching the scene.

I asked him, "Dude, are you drunk and have mistaken me for someone else?"

"I'm neither drunk, nor I mistook you. It's just a favour I want from you."

"I deny."

He came closer to me and whispered in my ear, "You remember the kiss of yesterday?"

I was stunned. Before I could say something, he started announcing, "Girls and boys, I wanna share an incident with y'all. Actually, yesterday I......."

"Stop! Stop! Stop! Let's go and take a pic outside."

He smiled cunningly and took me out.

With rudeness on my face, I asked, "Mr Steven, what you want now?"

"I just wanna have a picture with you."

"But why?"

"That shouldn't concern you. Just take a picture with me, rest assure, your pic won't go in wrong hands."

He put his arms around my shoulders and told me to smile lovingly for the picture. We took the picture.

Then he started doing something on his phone. I took a glance at it and saw that he was sending our picture to his dad with a caption

> "*'Dad! here is the pic of me with the girl I love. Now don't try to ship me with Dona again. And also, we're still young. We need to concentrate on our future career than involving in marriage issues'*"

and sent this message to his dad.

I shouted, "What are doing? You introduced me to your dad as your girlfriend?"

"Don't worry it won't affect you. I needed a shield to prevent myself from every day talks about marriage."

"So, you used me?"

"Or what else?"

"You jerk!"

I kicked him. Again on the same leg and went to the class.

9
The Revenge

I was so done with that guy's nonsense that I finally decided to revenge on him at any cost.

I went to my seat and started talking to Ava as she was sitting closest to me. Then after some time, Mia and Jane also joined us.

Suddenly Mia changed her expressions and said, "Oh, by the way, have y'all brought History assignment?"

Jane replied, "Of course, I have it in my locker. How can I forget his assignment? He's so outrageous that even a single mistake, he'll be very harsh on us. Then how can I think about forgetting his work."

Ava, "True. No one would dare to forget it."

Their talks about Mr. Torvald gave me a perfect idea to get revenge. His bag was just beside me.

When those three were busy talking, I silently started my 'Mission Revenge'. I started searching for his locker's keys in his bag. But even after searching more than 10 times, I wasn't able to find it. I asked Ava, "Hey, do you know where Steven keeps his keys in the locker?"

"Umm... it's usually hung on his locker only. He rarely takes out, 'cause there is no one to dare to touch his locker.

But.... why are you asking so?"

"Nothing, just asking out of curiosity."

I understood that just I needed to do was to go to the room of the student's locker and take out his key which might be hung there.

So I slowly and carefully left the class. After reaching the student's locker room, I tiptoed inside the room carefully. As I wanted, the key was there in his locker. I went to his locker and checked if his assignment of history is in the locker. Luckily, it was there. I thanked God for showering his luck on me and also apologized for invading other's privacy and framing him. But, it was he who framed me first. Because of him, I was suffering so much. Everyone in the school hated me because of him.

Well, after that I quickly took out the key after locking the locker. I was very happy at my victory till then. After that, I carefully went out.

I was on my way to class, celebrating my success in this. I was pretty sure that he won't be at mercy. Mr. Torvald would sue him.

But, suddenly Steven appeared from nowhere. I quickly hid the key in my pocket. I thought that he was gonna ask me something or suspect me. So, to avoid this suspicion, I greeted him in the first place, "Hii Steven"

But that jerk didn't reply to me. He just looked at me for few seconds and then went on his way. I too quietly went to the classroom. It was the first time when I wasn't arguing with him.

The starting 3 lectures were over. After that, it was recess time. We sat together to have lunch.

I was quietly having my lunch, when Steven said to Rason, "Hey, have you seen my locker key?"

My mouth automatically paused chewing the food. I was all frozen.

Rason replied, "No, I haven't."

Eden and Zeo together, "Neither we."

I was feeling quite nervous. And the same time, Jane asked looked towards me and said, "Hey what happened to you? Why you look pale?"

"Nothing, it's just I... I'm not feeling well."

"What happened? Are you fine?" asked Mia.

"Yea yea... I'm alright. Don't worry."

Quietly we had our lunch and went to the classroom.

The very next period was of History. But, I was feeling a bit disappointed in myself by then. I might be feeling bad 'cause I did such a thing for the first time. Also, somewhere I was scared that if Steven found who did that, I would be doomed.

Before I could even decide to correct my deed, the teacher entered the class. I was feeling anxious. But, I knew that I couldn't do anything. The teacher started calling our names according to our roll numbers.

The first call was for me, "Roll number 1, Amelia Somerson."

I went and submitted my assignment. After that roll number 2, then 3, 4,5,6,7, and so on.

After some time, Steven's chance came. Sir called out, "Roll number 56, Steven Young."

He directly said, " Sir I forgot to do my assignment."

"What did you say?", asked sir in a frightful manner.

"I forgot to do my work."

"You brat! Come out of your seat. Let me teach you a lesson."

He stood up and before going to him, he said to me in a low voice, "No matter what happens. Don't spill the truth.

Only dare to say if you wanna be canned, or worse, expelled.

I was damn shocked. 'He knew it. He knew everything. Still, he chose to save me. Why? And how he knew that I would stand to accept my fault.'

I wasn't able to understand anything.

Meanwhile, he went to Mr. Torvald. Mr. Torvald said, "Show your hand."

He showed his hand. Mr. Torvald took out his iron cane from the teacher's cupboard. He swished the cane and harshly hit on his palm. The marks were already visible from the first hit. He prayed that Mr. Torvald could stop in the first one only.

I was hearing everyone whispering, "How come Steven forget his work. He has always been the one who is first at submitting the work. Also, he has always been the topper of the class. How come this happened?"

I was full of guilt. I wasn't even able to keep this much guilt when Ava, said from behind, "It was just the first cane. Every student starts crying in his first hit and surrenders himself and some even leave the school. But Steven is so rigid. Well, I'm feeling bad for Steven. 'Cause 9 more hits are left."

After hearing this, I was feeling like I was the most devious creature on earth. I was regretting after doing this. I never thought that his punishment would be this much painful.

Mr. Torvald canned second time. In the second his skin was nearly torn apart 'cause the cane was made of iron with a hexagonal prism structure and sharp edges as well as corners.

The third hit gave him some wounds with blood.

I wasn't able to bear it anymore, but, the words of Steven were wandering in my mind.

The fourth hit gave him enough would that he could not use his hand for nearly a month or two.

By the fifth hit, his blood already started shedding. His hands were shivering with pain. Still, he was standing rigid.

Though Steven warned me I couldn't bear it anymore. I stood up from my seat and shouted in a loud voice, "Sir, I wanna say something."

I was just about to confess when Rason stood up and said, "Sir she's having a severe headache. May I take her to the infirmary?

I wasn't able to understand, why Rason said so.

Sir replied, "Alright. Take her. And you Steven 5 more are remaining."

Rason came outta his seat and said, "Let's go."

He held my hand headed off to the infirmary. I saw the 6th hit too. I was just about to cry. Before the 7th one, I was outta class.

I said to Rason, "Hey, what are you doing? Why you took me outta class."

"Right now be silent. I'll tell you everything. Just wait."

I silently obeyed him.

But, instead of the infirmary, he took me to the student's locker room.

He took me to Steven's locker. He took out a key from his pocket. The key was of Steven's locker. i wondered why he had that. It was with me.

He guessed my curiosity and answered, "This key fell on my feet from your pocket when you stood up to confess."

"Means you knew what I was going to say?"

"Not exactly. I just predicted but I became sure after the key fell down. And I needed to take an immediate step to save you. So I used this step to prevent you from spilling the truth."

"But why you didn't let me tell everything to sir?"

"Because Steven didn't want you to."

"How you know this?"

"In the last five minutes of recess, I took him out. I asked him why was he asking for his locker's key. He replied that someone has taken it out and his history assignment is in the locker. Then I asked if he has doubt on someone. He replied that he already knows who took it but he won't ask that person to give his keys back because he was curious why the person did that. I asked the name but he denied to tell. And after that, in the History period, when he was receiving the punishment I became sure that he didn't want the person to be punished. Hence, when you stood up, I framed all of this."

"He... He knew everything from the very start. Still, he expected me to confess it myself. What an idiot is he. Can't he see, how he is suffering by his decision?"

"I don't think that he's feeling like he's suffering. Instead he might be happy that he trusted the right person."

"Trust?"

"Yes! He trusted that you didn't mean to harm him in such a way. He trusted that you'll be honest even after doing such a mistake. He trusted that you're not a scheming girl. He trusted that you're a nice girl."

"But, why he think of me like this."

"He's really good at the judgment of people. And the moment you stood up to save him already proves his judgment right."

While we were talking about all this, Rason took out Steven's assignment and showed it to me. I looked at the assignment. I was stunned. He had done his assignment in such a perfect way that it was worth to be praised. His handwriting was so good and clear that I would really be lucky to do such work.

But, I suddenly realized what I did to him.

I started crying.

Rason tried to console me and said, "Don't cry okay."

In a sobbing voice, I said, "I'm such a devious person that I let him be punished in such a harsh way when the fault was entirely mine. And what's wrong with that teacher. Is he totally crazy? Who punishes a student in such a way?"

"Well. It's all over. After 5 minutes, the school will also get over. You'll meet him soon."

We waited for few minutes until school got over.

As the school bell rang, without even thinking about anything else, I ran to class.

I reached to the class and start looking for Steven. But he wasn't there. I asked Eden where Steven was. He replied that Steven went to the infirmary and he didn't take any of them for help.

Before he could continue to chat with me, I ran to the infirmary.

I entered the medical room. He was sitting there, waiting for the nurse. I ran to him and hugged him and started crying hard.

He hugged me back and said, "Don't cry."

I loosened the hug and then stood in front of him. I held his hand and looked at his palm.

It was bleeding. I was still crying.

I said, "Stupid boy... who said to take such a harsh punishment?"

"No one, I myself asked for it."

I calmed down myself for few moments while a nurse came and applied the medicine.

After she left the room, I said to him, "I'm sorry. I wanted to take revenge on you for everything you did. But I never expected this. I'm really very sorry."

"So how are you going to compensate me?"

"In any way you want?"

"Then don't regret later."

"I'm already regretting this much."

"Alright then. Go home right now. You'll get to know tomorrow."

"Alright, take care. Bye."

I moved out of the room and went home.

10
The Novel Reading

This all nonsense would have continued for a longer time if Jane had not gone to ask about the reason that teacher didn't come by then.

She soon came after asking and said, "Here is an announcement. Teacher is absent. You can do self study."

As all knew that students are not really this much obedient to do self study. Since there was no one to stop them that's why everyone started talking.

I was really unlucky that I had no one to talk to. Ava was angry with the argument with Rason.

Eden and Jane were talking to each other. Zoe and Mia were also busy in their so called romance.

The only person left was that crackhead. And, who would be so idiot to talk to him.

And to the worst, few moments later Dona came and stood beside me to talk to Steven who as on my right side.

Dona said in a very cheesy way, "Oh, Steven. Aren't you getting bored. Wanna hangout with me."

Steven ignored her words and took out a book to read.

Dona looked at the book and without even thinking, she said, "Oh, wow. I also like this book."

He said with a cunning smile, "Oh really. Can you even read this book."

"Of course. I can. I'm not illiterate."

"Oh, if that's the case. Then would like you to read the first line of the first chapter."

"Sure. Gimme,"

She tried to take from him but said, "Stop. I don't like people touching my things."

"But it's so far away. How will I read from here. Oh. We can do one thing. I can sit at the place of Amelia. She'll sit on other place for the meanwhile."

I would have agreed if there would have been an other girl. But it was her, who tried to hurt me on the second day of the school. Hence, I decided to deny.

But before I could say no to her. Steven replied on my behalf.

"She won't get up. And even if she wants to, I won't let her do it. How about this? She'll hold the book and you'll read."

"But why can she hold and I can't."

"I don't need to explain. You wanna read it to me or not."

"Ah! Alright."

Steven gave book to me and Dona tried to read. But she paused and said, "Hey, It's written in chinese. How can I read it?"

Steven replied, "Didn't you say that you like this book."

"I... I like it's english version."

"But it has never been translated to English."

I literally wanted to laugh out loud at that time but I controlled myself.

Then I thought that I can help him. 'Cause I can read read chinese and can translate it too. In this way, I could help to get rid of Dona.

I asked Steven, "How about I read?"
He made weird expressions and thought, 'Are you totally dumb. Didn't you hear, it's in Chinese language.'
I asked again, "Say. Can I try."
He replied in ignorant way, "As you wish."

I read the first line, in chinese, **"Nǐ hǎo, wǒ shì Xiá lù. Wǒ shì zhè běn xiǎoshuō de zuòjiā. Hěn gāoxìng rènshí nǐ, wǒ de dúzhě"**
Steven was stunned and thought, 'She can actually read it.'
I continued, "It's translation will be : *Hello, I'm Xia Lu (Shia Lu). I'm the writer of this novel. Nice to meet you my readers.*"

Ava also heard it.
I said to Steven, "Is the translation correct."
Steven replied in a surprised way, "Even the accent is perfectly the way a normal chinese have."
Ava complimented, "Amelia, you're too great!"
Jane also heard it. She said, "Amelia love learning new languages. It's not first time for me to hear any other language. But I really appreciate her for this."
Eden also complimented and said, "Amelia. You're awesome."
Mia and Zeo said, "Amelia, after Steven, we have seen only you to be fluent in other languages."

Before I could thank them for the compliment, Dona interrupted and said, "What's so great in this? Still Steven is better than Amelia. And also this doesn't prove that Amelia is amazing. She'll still be a fucking bitch! Nothing else."
Steven stood up and gave a death stare to Dona and said, "Don't dare to insult my benchmate."
Dona said, "Why are you caring so much about her? She isn't your girlfriend. Is she?"

"Even if she is not. But... She is my personal assistant. Her insult is indirectly my insult."

"Personal Assisstant! Steven, you're kidding me? I know that at such young age of 17, you've become a successful enterprenuer and you don't need any lousy PA like her."

I was surprised. I never knew that he is even capable to set up the bussiness that too at such a young age.

I was still recovering from the shock when Steven said to Dona, "It doesn't concern you. Now just *fuck off!*"

Dona went away without saying even a single word.

Rason said to Steven, "I'm sorry Steve, my sister causes you trouble everytime."

"It's fine. Not your fault. She's just a crazy creature and I know how to handle."

I replied said, "That's great that you know how. But make sure that she don't trouble me because of you again. This time I took my revenge for the last time."

Eden suddenly said, "Well, leave all this and tell me. Steve, when she became your PA."

Steven answered, "You think she's qualified to be my PA. She can't even be my servant."

Zeo asked,"Then why did you just now...."

"Just to avoid her. And also a pact is signed between me and this girl that she'll do as I said for a month."

"Why?", Asked Rason.

Steven replied, "Ask her."

At his reply, I literally wanted to curse him or kill him.

Mia asked, "What happened Amelia? Why you signed the pact with him?"

There was very less time to make up any excuse to escape. I had only one excuse which I could state. Hence, I said, "Umm.. actually. I... want to learn Spanish from Steven. As you know that I like learning new languages. Hence, I asked Steven to teach me Spanish. But, as y'all know that relations between me and Steven are not so good. So, I needed to do something for him in exchange of learning. That's why I agreed to work for him and listen to him for 1month."

After saying this, I gave a small hint to Rason to not tell anyone about yesterday and this whole thing going on.

Luckily, he didn't spill the beans.

Thank God! I was saved.

But this guy, Steven really sucked a lot. Everyday with him after that, were going like hell. Or worse than that.

Also that Dona would always come and pick on me because of that crackhead. But thanks to my dad that he let me in join karate class in middle school so now she's at least afraid of that.

11
The Test

One morning, I woke up late by chance. "Holy crap! I'll be late."

I woke up and get up from the bed and tried to get ready as soon as possible. I left all the morning household chores for that day and even skipped my breakfast. Luckily, I got ready on time. And even 10 minutes before the time, 'cause I skipped my breakfast.

Then I thought of going to school early, so, I took my car key and went to the car.

I really wanted to scream out loud when I noticed that the car engine has got some fault.

I dropped the idea of going by car. I decided to take taxi.

I took the taxi and reached there on time.

I stepped outta taxi. I stepped on mud. "Fuck!" I screamed.

Then I went inside the campus. While walking in the campus, I accidently slipped and fell down and hurt left elbow and right knee.

I didn't know why everything was going bad with me. I decided to once get in class and not to get out till the school gets over. Hence, I rushed to the classroom.

Once, I reached the classroom, I sat on my bench and sighed with relief when Mia came to me cand said, "Hey, are you done with the course of History that is coming in today's test?"

My heart sanked. I almost forgot about test. I didn't know what to do. I barely had 5 minutes left. The only thing I know was that I was about be doomed.

The bell rang. Before the commence of teacher, Steven and the other three guys also arrived.

Steven came and sat silently. I was wondering if he has studied something or not.

Rason said to Steven, "Hey, yesterday where we went to swimming, that place was awesome. How you found that place?"

"I was just sitting idle all the time so I thought of finding a big large and private swimming pool that we can rent. So I found that."

The way he was talking, clearly stated that he hadn't studied.

I was happy inside that I would not be the only person to get punished for less marks.

The teacher entered. We wished him good morning. I was highly hoping that he won't take our test but as soon as we sat doen, he said, "Students, take out all important accessories. I'll be distributing the paper soon."

I was totally surprised that he was so strict even in a class test that he would make the test papers with answer column for us.

We quietly took out the the pens. Teacher started distributing the paper. First bench was mine so of course, he started from our bench. He gave two papers to us. As I looked at the questions, I was literally about to get a minor heart attack. After reading the paper, it didn't seem that I've ever heard these terms before.

Soon the test papers were ditributed in the class. I wanted to cry. Even I was not able to sit properly. The knees of that crackhead would often hit my right knee as he was sitting on my right. And my right knee was injured. But I couldn't say a word or else Mr. Torvald would eat me up.

It was nearly two minutes and I wasn't writing anything. Steven noticed me and said, "What happened? Don't know the answers?"

"Does it concern you."

"At least write the name."

"What will I do after writing the name? Sit idle?"

"Maybe, but right now even you won't write your name, he will get to know that you know nothing."

His words made sense. I took my pen and wrote my name.

At that very moment, Steven exchanged the sheets. I whispered, "What are you doing."

He said in a very low voice, "Just stay silent."

After that he started writing in my paper and surprisingly in my handwriting. He completed my paper within 15 minutes and asked me to submit to the teacher.

I submitted it to teacher. After that, he started doing his test and completed his test also in 15 minutes. And after that, submitted to teacher.

On that day, I was really thankful to him. I didn't know why he helped me but what matters was that he helped me.

After some time, the test was over. Everyone submitted the test papers and then after the teacher was gone, they stretched their hands and felt relaxed.

Jane said, "Wow Amelia! You're amazing. You did the paper just in 15 minutes. You even broke the record of Steven who completes the paper at first always."

I didn't know what to say after all it was Steven who did my paper.

Before I could say or explain anything, Steven held my hand and made me stand up. I yelled, "What are you doing?" Without even giving a response, he took me outta class. Then after, he took me straight to infarmary. And made me sit down.

I asked again, "What are you doing?"
He put finger on his lips and said, "Shhh.. Be quiet."
He took out the antiseptic cream, cotton and occlusive bandages. He asked me to show my elbow to him first. I showed him.
He applied the cream and then rubbed with cotton and covered the wound.
Then he knelt down and did the same for the knee.
It was the first time that I was feeling that he's not that bad.
I suddenly said, "Thank you."
He looked up and said, "For what?"
"For helping me in first aid."
"Tch.. you think too much. This I'm doing because I don't want you to make this excuse to escape from the work."
"Oh really! Then what about your help in test?"
"You really think it was for free?"
"Of course not. I know you will make me compensate for your help."
"Smart enough."
"Hey, by the way, how you you copied my handwriting so perfectly."
"Because you wrote your name on that paper. So, I got to know your way of forming the letter , so I wrote all paper in your handwriting."

Though, I hated him but I should really say that he was an extremely perfect in nearly every feild.

He could even copy anyone's handwriting so easily.

Then I remember that I need to compensate for his help. So, I asked, "Well, how you want me to compensate?"

"You need to work me for 6 months now."

"What the hell are you talking about."

"Yea, that's what the condition is. If you don't do it. Then I'll tell the sir that you forced mt to do your paper or else you'll bring the boys to beat me up."

He was damn disgusting. But then I thought that if he likes playing around so much then why not to play a game with him.

Then I said, "Alright, just go and say all this. You have written whole paper in my handwriting. Who will believe? Just and say whatever you wanna say. Even if you're innocent, no one's gonna believe you. And in these cases I'm much better in acting than you."

Steven was shocked. He was frowning hard. And this was what making me happy.

Then he said, "You... are really lucky this time."

I smiled cunningly and then stood up, thanked him for helping me and went to the class.

12
Unexpected Shock!

I went to the class and sat with a victorious smile. After a while, Steven also came, but this was the first time I wasn't disgusted by him. After all it was my first time that I won against him. That day went pretty well. Though the starting of day was the worst but after few hours my good luck started. True said, "God balances both Good and Bad like that in YIN YANG."

I went to home and was feeling really happy. That was really a very nice day indeed. I studied after coming to home and then cooked the food and slept.

On the next morning, at 6:30AM when I was sleeping, someone started blowing car horn. I covered my ears with pillow. But the car driver was bloeing horn continuously. It was freaking killing me. I finally woke up and went to the balcony to ask the driver to stop blowing horn.

As I looked down in the balcony, I realised that the car driver was none other than Steven. I shouted from balcony but the car horn was covering my sound. So, I went downstairs, opened the main gate of the apartment and then stood beside his car and after that he finaly stopped blowing the horn. I asked him to get outta car and after he got outta car, I held his hand took upstairs in my flat. On my way, I apologised all the neighbours who were disturbed by him.

After taking him inside, I shut the door with a lound bang sound of the door. Then I yelled, "Steven!! Are you insane? Can't you have a bit sense of conscience? Why you came here? And even if you came, who told you to blow the horn?"

"Firstly, just see with whom you're talking to and lower your voice. Secondly, I didn't know your flat number so I blew the horn, I only knew address of your apartment."

"And why you came here?"
"Because... I... I... want you to make coffee for me."
"You know what Steven... Soon I'll be going to jail."
"Wow. Now you're criminal?"
"I wasn't but I think I will be. Police will soon arrest me in case of murder of a crackhead."
"Oh! That we will see later. First make me coffee."
"I've no time!"

I turned around to got to bathroom for getting ready when suddenly I heard a voice from Steven's phone, "_Alright, just go and say all this. You have written whole paper in my handwriting. Who will believe? Just and say whatever you wanna say. Even if you're innocent, no one's gonna believe you. And in these cases I'm much better in acting than you._"

It took me no time to realise that it was recording of my voice. The recording stopped and then he kept his phone in pocket and then said, "I'm afraid that if I give this recording to Mr. Torvald, you'll be doomed."
"You're threatening me or warning me?"
"You can think in either of these ways."
"Mr.Steven Young. I swear, you'll regret it."
"We'll see that later. first make a cup of coffee for me."

I had no other options. Hence, I agreed to make coffee for him. I went to the kitchen. He followed me to the kitchen. I said, "Can't you just sit and wait?"
"Who knows if you'll poison me to death."
"I really wish to."
"You said something?"
"Nothing. I'm making coffee."

I opened the kitchen cupboard. It was tightly closed so it took me a bit of effort in opening which caused pain in my elbow. My expressions were telling enough that my injured elbow and knee were paining. He stopped watching from kitchen door, came inside the kitchen and took the cup from my hand and then said, "You're even feeling pain in opening the cupboard, how were you supposed to drive to school. Thank to your destiny that I came."

I realised that the reason he came of course could not be so lame. He came to take me to the school. But too cold to accept his kindness. I smiled at him while he was still looking at my elbow seriously. I think it was my first time to look at him so closely with a pleasant smile on my face. While I was continuously watching him, he suddenly looked at me and said,"I know I'm handsome enough but stop looking at me."

I realised and embarrased on my stupidity and then said, "Don't flatter yourself too much. Who wanna look at a crackhead. Now you can wait, I'll make coffee."

I was about take the cup from him but he did not give me and said, "Leave this to me. I can't rely on you. You might not even know the difference between sugar, salt and white poison, and will kill me by adding wrong ingredients. You better go dress up. I'll make it."

It's said that if the help comes without conditions, just accept it taking them as the result of good deeds in previous specially when the person helping is someone like Steven. Hence, I lent my kitchen to Steven and went to bathroom to get ready.

After some time. I got ready and went to dining room. I was surprised to see that coffee and breakfast was ready on the dining table for me. Steven was washing rest of the utensils. I went to the chair and sat and waited for Steven to come and dine with me.

After five minutes, he came, sat and the chair and said, "Haven't started yet?"
"I was waiting for you."
"You should have started. I'm already habitual to eat alone."
"It's okay. I'm also habitual of eating alone. So, let's dine together."

We ate the breakfast and then I went to school with Steven. When we reached the school, I said, "Hey, drop me here only. Don't take me to main gate, 'cause if people will see us together, they might guess something wrong."
"As I remember correctly, few days ago, I took you to school in your car. You remember."
"I remember it well and after that I got an enemy. So, better stop here."
"Let me see who dares to gossip about me."

He didn't listened to me and then accelerated the car straight to the parking. There were many students watching his car. Getting outta his car and standing in front of those lovesick girls was like getting outta castle and standing in front of the army of enemy.

As Steven got outta car, girls started staring him and admiring him. I did not have guts to get out 'cause I would be dead meat if I would do so. But as soon as Steven got off from the car, he came to my side and asked me to get out. I denied. So, he held my hand, took me out of car and closed the door.

Every girl standing there was watching me and was stunned 'cause I was the first girl ever to sit on the front seat of his car, plus he was the driver. I was having bad intuitions that now those girls would plan to murder me on the spot or poison to the death in lunch break. But that crackhead, Steven would not hear a word even if I try to explain. He kept holding my hand and we soon reached near class.

I removed his foregrip off my hand and yelled at him, "What the hell are you doing you freaking wanna be killed today?"
"You really wanna argue with me. I helped you but still greatfull you are yelling at me. Who you think you are?"

I silently entered the class because it was in vain to argue with him. As I entered the class, I sat silently on my seat. He also entered the class. I was surprised that on thet following day, he didn't go outta class. I was about to ask him reason when the other three guys also came in the class. Jane, Ava and Mia also came.

The four occupied the seat of Rason and started talking and we four were on my seat.
We were having fun in light talking when Dona came to us.

He looked at me fiercely and then looked towards Steven and said, "Steven! How can you bring her with you? She's just your classmate and your benchmate. How can you be so close to a new girl so easily."
"I think so it must not concern you that with whom I am and with whom I'm not."
"Why should I not? I want to know what's the relationship between you and her."
I couldn't bear to create any misunderstanding so I got up and said, "Dona, I think you're mistaken. He was just

helping me."

"Just help! This all is what you call just help? Don't be oversmart in front of me. You bitch!"

She was just about to slap me. But before she could take her hand to my face or I could defend, Steven grabbed her hand and made her hand down forcefully.

I could see the anger in his eyes. He said, "Dare not to touch my girlfriend!"

She exclaimed, "Girlfriend!"

I was in a state of shock.

Everyone stopped talking in the class.

I wasn't able to believe what I heard. There were expression of shock on faces of all people, specially Dona, Ava, Rason, Jane, Eden, Mia and Zeo.

I was so confused and stunned that I didn't know why he said so.

13

Girlfriend?

---♡---

Dona was smart enough to not believe so easily. She said, "I don't believe. Proof?"

Steven came held my neck and pulled me closer and kissed me! I wasn't able to react anything. And surprisingly I wasn't resisting.

After a moment, I gained the concsience and I pushed him back. He acted casually and said to Dona, "Now you believe.?"

"She pushed you back. I've clearly seen."

"So you want her to keep kissing me in front of so many people?"

Dona looked at me and said, "Are you really his girlfriend."

As he kissed me, so he must be a bit responsible and also if I denied, who knows if he would have given that recording to teacher.

Hence, I replied to her boldly, "Yes. I am. Any problem?"

She said, "Amelia, I think you've forgotten that I gave you warning that not to get to close to Steven."

"And as I remember, I also warned to not patience or else, you've already seen my power and skills in Karate."

"You're threatening me."

"It's a threat or warning, it's up to how you wanna take it."
"You'll regret it."
"We'll see later."
She went away, murmuring something bad. I smiled and then looked at Steven. He was smiling at me in an impressive way. Maybe because he never expected this response.

Mia asked, "Hey, you're really in relationship?"

I replied, "Of course not. Do I look like to be so easy girl? It was just to get rid of her."

Zeo said, "Amelia, the way you spoke was something worth praising. You were really so bold."

"Thanks!", I replied.

Steven was still looking at me in an impressive way. I waved my hand his hand in front of his eyes and when he shook his head, I said, "What happened? Impressed by my acting?"

"Hah! Don't flatter yourself so much. People get impressed by something which is impressive."

"Wasn't I impressive just now?"

"You wish!"

"How rude."

"I am. So?"

"If a curse would work then I would really like to give you one."

"What curse?"

"That you loose your that part of brain which you use to blackmail people, act cold and think highly of yourself."

"Even if it happened, I will still be better than you and will be able enough to at least keep you down in front of me."

"So overconfident."

"Just a fact."

While we were just making fun of each other, I noticed that other six, standing and watching us and smiling at us.
Ava said,"You both look so cute with each other. That's so sweet. Perfect couples."
I and Steven exclaimed together, "Who are couples!"
Jane laughed and said, "Alright. Now stop it. Teacher is about to come."
All went to their seats. And after that I was feeling shy about the kiss and the way I talked to Dona. Then Steven said, "Thanks."
I said frankly, "Oh, please! Words like thank you, sorry, excuse me don't suit your cold and bossy attitude. And anyways, I did it to pay off the help that you gave me previously."
"You think too highly of yourself. When I helped you?"
"You know it yourself clearly. I don't need to tell." then I smiled and start reading a book.

As the bell rang, it was history period so Mr. Torvald arrived. He had the results of previous test in his hands. We wished him morning and then sat down.
He was looking happy which was really good for us that he would not scold us unnecessarily.
He said, "Students. I'm very happy that this you didn't let me down in your first test of this session. Here are your checked test papers. Everyone has passed with more than 70%. And now let's talk about the toppers of the class. There are 4 people who scored full in the test. Amelia, Jane, Rason and Steven. These students have performed the best and scored full marks."

I was supposed to happy for the marks but I wasn't because it wasn't me who did the test. It was Steven. So the credit was of him.
I was thanking him by heart.

Then teacher announced, "So, according to the results, I want to make Amelia and Steven as the class representatives as their answers were a bit more up to the point than the other two. And also, Jane and Rason, you both are deputy Class Representatives. Is it fine?"

Jane raised her hand said, "Excuse me sir. Actually I want to withdraw from this position."

Mr. Torvald asked the reason so she told about her recent co curricular activities because of which she would have no time for class.

Then teacher asked, "Then... whom to make deputy class represenitive."

Rason said, "Sir I have a suggestion. You can count on Ava. She is really interested and also capable to take this responsibility. Also we both are benchmates. Hence, we can cooperate well."

Ava was stunned and thought, 'Is this guy calling for troubles for me.'

Teacher looked at Ava and with satisfaction, "Alright then Ava, you'll be the deputy c.r."

She had no choice other than accepting the responsibility given to her as Rason had given all possible reasons using which she could have make excuse but she hadn't any. Hence, she agreed.

She sat down and gave a death stare to Rason, while Rason was smiling cunningly.

As the period got over, Ava yelled, "Rason Maxwell! Are you tired of this life. You know I don't like all these, then why you took my name?"

"So that you'll not be able to do all those stuffs which you used to do like talking continuously, coming late, bunking class, etc. etc."

"Why you meddle around my business? You have any

problem with me?"

"Finally you realised that I do have."

"Rason! At this moment if only it was included in human rights, I would have killed you. Such an unscurplous guy."

"Are you still so dumb to understand who's unscurplous here?"

"You.... leave it. It's just in vain to talk to you."

"But still keep chattering whole day and eating my brain up."

"I do and I will."

Eden saw this and said, "Are they again flirting."

Rason looked at him and said, "Eden. Is there something wrong with your brain. Who would flirt with a monkey."

Ava exclaimed, "Monkey!"

Rason said, "Someone who always keep chattering, roaming here and there around, don't you know what we call that?"

Ava said, "Rason. Now just shut your mouth or else I....."

Before Ava could complete her sentence, Chemistry teacher arrived and said, "What's happening here?"

Mia said instantly, "Ma'am nothing. It's just we were talking about our new monitors."

"Alright. Settle down fast."

Luckily, both were saved by Mia.

Finally the second and the third period also ended. In the lunch time, teacher called Steven for discussion about the sports. So he skipped the recess.

We all collected to have lunch. While we were having lunch, Eden said, "Steven will be skipping today's lunch. Won't he will feel hungry afterwards?"

"Maybe he'll cook himself lunch when he gets home." said Rason.

"But does he knows how to cook." asked Jane.

I was eating my lunch so without thinking I just said, "He can. And he really cooks very well."

Ava asked, "How you know?"

"He cooked breakfast for me today and made coffee." I split it out while eating and didn't realised what I was saying.

I suddenly realised what I said and stopped eating and looked at them. They all were staring at me with expression of surprise. They all said line wise.

Jane - "He sat with you."

Eden - "He drove you to school."

Mia - "He claimed you his girlfriend."

Zeo - "He kissed you."

Ava - "He cooked for you."

Rason, "Leave all this, he even bore the punishment for her."

Rason told that incident to all of them. All were even more surprised.

I was only thinking one thing after that, 'I'm doomed.'

I ate the lunch as fast as I could an than tried to leave place. But Eden stopped me and said, "Wait, I've a question for you. Can I ask. Don't worry I won't think something bad."

"Alright. Say."

"What do you think of Steven. I mean how you think he is like?"

"He... he is a bit helpful but at the same time, a troublemaker. He is good by heart a bit but at the same time he's devilious by mind. He knows how to respect feelings but at the same time he disrespects my each and every words. He..."

Steven came and said, "Is she saying something ill about me?"

I noticed him and stood up from chair and said, "I don't have so much time to waste to talk about you."

Then I silently but nervously left the place.
The day was hectic but was nice.
I was glad that soon our deal was about to be at end because 1 month would get over in 3 weeks.

14
He became the cold one again

Days went by. Finally the day came when it was my last day of deal with him to work for him. I came and sit happily that from the following I would not need to work for him anymore. I was sitting calmly. Soon Steven came. I said to him, "So, from today onwards I'll not work for you, do your tasks anymore."

He said, "I know. And I always fulfill my promise. So from today onwards you're free. But not totally. You still need to act like my girlfriend in front of Dona as well as my father."

"Alright! No problem, as long as you won't disturb my life anymore."

"So, I was just merely a disturbing element of your life?"

"What else you think you are. But since, you're so sincere with your words then I would also not go back on my words. I never thought of helping the person I hate the most. But your sincerety I am willing to help you."

"You hate me at this extent?"

"Of course, I do. But don't worry. Though I hate you the most but then too I know to keep my words."

"Alright then. Thanks. I think I would not need your help in pretending, since you hate me so much."
"Hey wait, I..."
He just ignored my words and went away.
I mumbled, "Weirdo!"

He was looking a bit different. His expressions were dull and he was looking like he's upset by anything. We just had our classes and then went to home. For whole day, we didn't talk to each other. He kept his long face all day. I just quietly went to home.

It continued for nearly a week, we didn't talk to each other. I, then felt that my life started to get boring again. Though, I did not have to drive for him when he wants. Though, I did not have to fill water for him. Though, I did not have to wake up early because of him, though now there was no one to irritate me but I think I was missing all these things.

I realised that I was happy and lively by all these things. I gave a deep thought on what I actually think of him. I realised that I don't hate him this much. When I clearly thought about all the things, I realised that though he would irritate me sometimes but he would not abuse me. He even helped me multiple times. Hence, I decide to be friends with him.

Next day, I went to school early. I waited for him. After 10 minutes, he came. I looked at him and put my bag aside to make a seat for him. He sat. I greeted him, "Hey, what's up!" But he gave no reply. Instead, he took out the text book and started studying.
I tried to gain attention and said, "Hey, I'm talking to you."
He kept his book again in the bag and then looked at me and said, "Since you have nothing to do then study or roam around the corrider. But, don't disturb others."

"What's wrong with you Steven? Why aren't you talking to me?"

"Is there anything to talk about? And also now we have nothing to do with each other, then what to talk about. Now excuse me, *classmate*."

Then he went away.

I didn't know why but it really hurt when he said classmate. I was feeling like stranger. The guy who was so frank, irritating element and a helping around became stranger as soon as the deal ended.

Soon the class started. It was period od Lucy ma'am, our English teacher. Just before the ma'am arrived, he also came and sit silently. We wished the teacher. She gave her lesson and went away. Same happened in second and third lecture. He was still silent. By then, his silence was sucking me. But I couldn't do anything.

Soon the school day ended. I asked Rason to wait for me after the school. Hence, Rason waited for me on the parking area when everyone went away. I then went to him and said, "Can we go somewhere like cafe?"

"Sure. Let's go. Here's a cafe nearby. Let's go there."

"Okay."

We got into our respective car and then went to cafe. After getting there, Rason ordered two cups of Latte. We the seats. Then he said, "Yes, say. What help you want?"

"Umm... actually, don't you think that Steven is acting weird since one week?"

"Is he? I don't think so."

"Rason. Be serious."

"I'm serious. He has always been like this. Yes you can say that before this one week, he was different for nearly a month. Now he's again the same guy he used to be."

"Is it?"
"If you don't believe me, then just go and ask any person in the class. Although we never mentioned but the way he changed for one month was surprise for all of us. You know before you came, he never talked to girls. But after you came, he even started talking to Jane, Ava, Mia and few other girls sometimes. He never smiled. We rarely used to see him smiled before you came. But after you came, he became totally a different person. You know why no girl in the campus hate him? Because he never picked on them. He would not even give a glance on them. And even no one dared to do something to offend him. Except for me, Eden and Zeo, no one in this school had guts to offend him or make fun of him. After us, it's only you have guts to tackle him and to even argue him, hit him, shout at him, offend him and even set him up. Still he was so tolerant towards you."

I was totally surprised by this. Then I asked Rason, "If the things are like that, then why didn't you tell me earlier?"
"It's because if we would have told you earlier, we were afraid that you will start keeping distance from him. Everyone of us was noticing it silently but none of us told you 'cause we were happy that he is changing in a positive manner. But I can't say what happened recently that he is again like that. Do you have any clue that what has happened to him?"
"I don't think so. When we last talked he just asked me that if I hate him this much then I agreed so he just said, no need to help him anymore and then he went away saying me goodbye. What a weird guy, right?"
He made an expressions like 'are you serious' and then said, "Dude, what else you expect after that?"
I was a bit puzzled by his words and expressions so I asked,

"What you wanna say?"
"You still want me to say? You didn't understand it yet? Leave it. I can't help you in this. You need to understand this yourself if you wanna know him well. I can just say that how come you both are noobs in this matter?"
"What matter? What I need to figure out?"
"I can't help you in this. It depends on you that how much you understand. Alright, now I shall take my leave. Bye and drive safely."
"Alright, bye."

Honestly, I didn't understand even a single word of what he said. I think I was really bad at understanding a person like him. But it wasn't my fault anyways. Who could understand that person. But one thing I already understood that without him around me, it was no fun. I had no one to talk to, no one to argue with and no one to pick on.
Hence, that evening I went home and started thinking about how to make him speak with me again. Then I came up with an idea. I smirked and appreciated myself for that idea and started jumping on the sofa on which I was sitting. But I suddenly lost my balance and fell down. Thank god a carpet was there or else I would have hurt my injured parts again.

But I was just excited to repeat those things once again. I had a sound sleep to wake up early next morning.

15
Just Stranger Treatment

The next morning when I woke up, I was already very much excited. I did all my household chores and then rushed to school.

As I went to the class, I waited for Steven to come. He arrived, placed his bag on the bench, and then went away without saying a word. I was getting both frustrated and upset by his this behavior.

But, according to my plan, I knew that it wouldn't last long. After he went outside with his squad, I silently looked for the key of his locker in his bag. But I didn't find it. Then I suddenly remembered that Steven put his keys in his locker only. I walked to the students' locker room. I silently went to his locker and as expected, the key was there on his locker only.

I quickly took out the key and hid it in my pocket and went outside as if nothing happened. The first period was of English.

He also came into the class. As he sat, I chuckled and then looked straight. I was waiting when him to find out that the key was missing and then talk to me about that.

In the whole English period, nothing happened. But I didn't

get disappointed as there was still a whole day left.

The next period was Sports. I went outta class to get to the playground earlier with Ava. After few minutes the whole class arrived. Then I suddenly realized that I forgot to bring the water bottle. I headed off to class again to bring my bottle.

As I was walking in the corridor, I tripped and fell exactly on the knees where there was already a wound. I screamed a bit, "Ouch! Not again."

I was trying to get up when I saw Steven coming towards me. He came and stood in front of me and gave me his hand. I smiled as I was happy that he was helping me but as I was about to hold his hand, he moved his hand aside and then said, "Not your hand. The keys."

I was puzzled for a second but then understood. Still, I chose to pretend as I know nothing and then said, "What keys?"

"I don't have much time. Gimme the keys."

I took the keys out of my pocket and gave them to him. He took the keys and away while I kept shouting, "Hey, at least help me to stand up. I'm still injured and am not able to stand up. Hey, are you listening? Hey?"

I kept shouting until his appearance was completely faded from my sight.

I shouted, "Such a jerk."

At the same time, Zeo came from nowhere. He came to me and gave me his hand and helped me to stand up. I thanked him and then went to the class to get my bottle. Then I straight went to the playground.

At that time I wanted to cry a lot. The guy who used to pick on me, who took the punishment on my behalf, who helped me when my wounds were still in a bad condition, was now treating me like a stranger.

I didn't play in the whole sports period and just sat in the corner as the blood was again over my knee.

After the sports period, I went to the class with the help of Jane. It was chemistry class. Thankfully I like Chemistry or else my mood would have been the same.

The class started though it was tough to concentrate while sitting with a person who treated you as a stranger suddenly but anyways I did concentrate and after the class, our chemistry teacher said, "Amelia, it's recess time. I wanna have a talk to you. Come to the staffroom with me."

I nodded and followed the teacher.

The teacher took me to the staffroom. There was no other teacher.

I asked the teacher, "Yes ma'am. How can I help you."

MA'am turned on the computer and showed me the recording of me taking out the keys of the locker of Steven.

Then she said, "What is this? You know it very well that you're not allowed to touch other student's locker."

I was feeling very scared. I didn't know what to say. I was about to cry when suddenly Steven entered the staffroom. I was stunned.

He said, "Ma'am I was the one who asked her to bring my keys."

I was surprised that he was lying to save me.

Then ma'am said, "Steven! What is this? Previously also when we caught her you gave the same excuse. We warned you earlier also."

I was shocked and stared at him. I never knew that he had helped hike this.

Ma'am scolded us a little and then let us go by giving the last warning.

As we came out of the classroom, I asked him, "Hey, thanks for the help. But, why you helped me."

"That doesn't concern you. But remember not to do it or else I'm not responsible for it. And yes don't overthink. I helped you because you once helped by pretending with me."

He started walking. I held his hand and then asked him, "Are you angry with me."

He stared at me and then said, "Who are you that I need to get angry at you."

"Then why are you treating me like a stranger? How did I offend you?"

"Firstly, you were never a friend of mine. So, I must treat a stranger as a stranger. And also we are even now."

"How can you say that?"

"You must be happy. You hate me the most and now you've finally got rid of me."

"Hey, that day, I didn't mean that."

"No need to explain to me. It doesn't concern me."

"Steven! I just said it casually that I hate you and you took it so seriously. How can you change into completely a different human just in a night? What's your problem? Can't you be a bit soft? Why are you so rude always?"

"Whatever."

He shrugged and went away.

I wanted to stop him but for me, my self-respect is the most important. Hence, I let him go.

I wanted to share it with Jane, but I knew that she had many family problems. Also, I didn't want that Jane and Mia get bad relations with Eden and Zeo because of me. Hence, I only had one person to share all this. Ava.

It was recess time, I quietly went to the cafeteria and asked Ava to come with me. I took her to the corner and asked her to come with me to my house on that day.

She agreed.

After that, recess ended and the other classes started. After school ended, I took her to my home in my car as she came by taxi that day.

As we reached my house, I offered her to sit on the sofa.

"Want anything? Snacks?"

"Nah! Oh yea, lemme call my mum and tell her that I'm at your house."

Before she could call her mom, her mom called her.

She picked up the call and said, "Hey mom."

"Hello, sweetheart. Actually, your aunt's sick. So, I need to go out of town. I'll return in two days, till that can you please live at our relatives' place."

She frowned and said, "Mom, no! I don't like living with them. It'll be better if I live alone."

"But dear, try to understand. I'm worried about you."

"Mom no. I won't go to their house."

I understood the problem and suggested to Ava, "Ava why don't you live with me for these two days? I live alone anyways."

She got excited and said, "Really! wait lemme ask my mom."

She asked her mom and her mom agreed also said that she'll come to my house to give her the clothes for two days.

Till her mom arrived, I prepared the snacks with the help of Ava.

Soon her mom came and gave her the clothes, pecked on her forehead, and headed off to the car.

After she went away, we finally rested and sat on the couch, and sighed.

Ava suddenly stood up and looked at me.

"What happened?" I asked with widening eyes.

"Sit straight with me."

Without even questioning, I obeyed her.

After we both sat on the couch, she looked at me suspectingly and said, "Didn't you want to discuss something with me?"

I suddenly recalled why I actually called her.

She put her hands on my shoulders and said, "Say, what happened?"

I moved my here and there and to lie and said, "Nothing. Leave it."

"Aren't you gonna tell me?"

"Actually, I..."

"Wait, lemme guess. It's about Steven?"

"How you know?"

"Is it hard to guess? Steven has again become the way he used to be before you came. That clearly means that something has happened between you two."

"Actually, in recent days he's weird. I mean, he's much colder than he usually is. Especially he's treating me like a stranger."

Ava sighed and said, "Dude! You're upset because of that guy. C'mon, you're upset like he's your boyfriend."

"Ava, do you know what you're saying?"

"Of course I know. Always remember. There are many other people who love and care for you. You should not neglect others just for one person. Leave thinking about him and chill. Let him regret. If he's ignoring you, then you ignoring you, then you make him feel the double of what you're feeling to make him regret."

"But it was my fault. I said to him rudely that I hate him."

"Then what about him. Did he treat you like a human, classmate, or friend in the whole month? He always gave you different tasks and works."

"But he helped me too."

"Even if he did, he must be open to others. Not others but at least with himself. If you really want my suggestion then I would suggest not to let yourself down for him. I've given my opinion. Rest, the decision is yours."

Her words made sense. I thought about it and finally decided to let him do whatever he wants. I also decided not to be sad because of him and ignore him the way he was.

16
Ava and I Became close

---◦♡◦---

After having some snacks, we sat on the couch again and started talking to each other to know each other well. She stared at me and then said, "Hey Amelia, why you live here alone? Where are your parents?"
"Actually my father stays busy in the job so he would often stay in the office. He comes only on Sundays and sometimes Friday or Saturday."
"Oh, I can relate. The same used to be with my grandpa. My dad told me. By the way, your mother?"
"My mom... umm... she... died in an accident when I was twelve."
"Oh, I'm really sorry to ask you this."
"It's okay. You didn't know anyways."
"Hmm... *suddenly jumping* Oh yea! I almost forgot. When you went with the teacher, Mr. Torvald came into the class and gave some home assignments."
She went to the study table, took out a notebook and came and sit again, and handed me the notebook to take a look at the assignment.
I read the assignment and said, "It's about the music."
Ava sighed and said, "That's why I'm exhausted just by

looking at it."
"Why to worry, when you have me?"
"You like music?"
"I love music!"
"Awesome!"
"Yea, you know since I was a little girl, I've been always interested in music, dance, and sports a lot. Learning academics is also included."
"You're great Amelia."
"Haha, Thanks."
"Oh by the way, though I don't have much knowledge about singing still, I have an idol."
"Who?"
"The Secret Pheonix"
"Wow! He's your favorite also?"
"Yours too?"
"Yep. Since I've entered my teenage, he has been my one and only crush and Idol crush."
"Oh wow! But the only problem is he doesn't show his face at all. He would always put on the mask and goggles. "
"Yea, that's what sucks the most. Anyways, we can't do anything about it. He'll show his face when he wants to."
"Yea. Oh well. Let's start off with the homework."
Both of us started doing the homework and after finishing it, we were finally free, hence we cooked the dinner and after doing the lunch we enjoyed ourselves a little, did some net surfing and then went to sleep.

 The next day, as I entered the class, I was determined to do as told by Ava and I did the same. I just didn't care when he would come and go. I just put my bag on the seat and rushed to the corridor to catch up with Ava who was waiting for me. I think, at that time, I and Ava were in the same boat. We both have rivals with whom we would sit and both suck.

Well, I didn't care much about it anymore and then rushed outta class. As I turned to take a right turn, I bumped into Steven. I just took a glance at him and just as we say to strangers, I said to him, "I'm sorry." And then rushed to the way I was going to. It was a bit awkward but I did it anyway.

Ava secretly watched by hiding behind a wall and then when I went that way, she herself appeared in front of me and gave me a thumbs up. I winked at her and said, "I'm a weed. No one dares to mess up with me."

And then I flipped my hair.

Soon the bell rang and we went to our class. The first period was of mathematics. Even before the teacher arrived, I took out the book and notebook and started doing my favorite part of maths, Trignometry.

But that was so unlucky of me that I got stuck in the first question itself.

Though the maths genius was just sitting beside me, for me, he was air.

Hence, I turned back and asked Ava if she could solve it. She sighed and said, "Dude, if I were capable to do the maths myself, why would I not score full?"

Rason sighed and said to me, "Amelia, you should know that you must ask the people who've got some senses."

I knew that he was indirectly talking about Ava. She looked at him with narrow eyes and said, "You dare to speak it by facing me."

"Did I say that I was talking about you?"

He smirked and chuckled. Before they could get into a fight, I said, "Wait! Sort your matters outta class. Can anyone of you solve this?"

Rason made his hand forward and said, "Gimme the notebook. Lemme try."

Rason tried to solve the question but unfortunately, after trying five times, he failed. He made a tch sound, sighed, and gave my copy back saying, "I'm sorry Amelia. I wasn't able to do it."

I nodded a bit and said, "No worries. Thanks for trying. I'll ask the teacher when she'll teach this lesson."

He smiled warmly and then started reading the book.

Ava said in a teasing manner, "Umm... Amelia. Someone said it right. You should know that you must ask a person who've got senses."

Rason's warm expressions turned into cold ones again and he looked at her and rolled his eyes saying, "Fucking Idiot!"

Ava widen her eyes and yelled, "What did you say?"

He continued while putting his eyes on the book, "Now a deaf too."

"STOP!" I said in a loud voice. They looked at each other in anger and then turned their faces in opposite ways. But they both were pretty cute like that.

I chuckled and looked in front again. Steven coughed a little to show me a sign that maybe he could help me with that question. But, as I was determined to ignore him and just treat him as air, I didn't respond to his cough.

He finally gave up and said, "Maybe, I can solve it."

I averted and said, "No thanks. But I don't like taking help from strangers."

He widened his eyes with surprise and then looked in front to show ignorance.

The teacher arrived and the class started. As the school time was over, I was totally exhausted. I quickly rushed to the home with Ava.

After reaching home, I jumped on the couch and just laid down as usual.

After some time, we changed into casuals and then ate soya sticks and drank milk for the snacks. The following day, we didn't get any assignments to do. Hence, we started playing and talked about our life in middle school.

We laughed a lot. When we were just talking about our idol, 'the secret Pheonix.

Then suddenly my dad called me. I picked it up with excitement and said, " Hello dad!"

"Hey, my sweety. What are you doing?"

"Nothing dad, just a friend came home so just chatting with her. What's up with you dad?"

"Dear, as usual, busy with the work. Don't even get time to see my love for two minutes. You must be angry with me right."

"Of course not dad. After all, you're doing this for me."

"That's so sweet of my daughter. Well, today, I called you for urgent work."

"Yep, I'm all my ears."

"Actually, dear. We need to transfer again."

I widen my eyes with shock and said, "What!"

"I'm sorry dear. I know it's really very fast this time but, we can't do anything. I'll come home the day after tomorrow."

"Al-alright dad," I said in a low voice and then hung up the call.

Ava, who was sitting beside me asked, "Hey, what happened?"

As I moved my lips a bit to tell her, I started crying.

She held me in her arms and said, "Dude! Don't cry. Just tell me what happened."

I wanted to control myself but I wasn't able to.

After a few minutes, I finally stopped crying. She put her hand on my cheeks and said, "Now tell me. What's wrong?"

I said while continuously sniffing, "I-that- I- my dad- my

dad- he called me and said- he- he- is gonna- he- transfer again."

Ava looked at me with a confused expression and then said, "Lemme bring you a glass of water. Drink that and then calm down. After that say whatever you wanna say. 'cause I'm not able to understand what you're saying. I just heard, your dad, transfer."

Then she went to the kitchen and brought water for me.

I drank water, calmed myself down and after that, I told her in a low voice, "My dad called me to tell me about our transfer. I and my dad are going to States."

"What?"

"Yep! And my dad is coming home the day after yesterday."

"Then why don't you pursue him to let you stay here?"

"He won't agree. After all, I'm his only family. He can't just easily leave me here."

"What should we do now?"

"Nothing. I can't hurt my dad in any way by arguing with him."

"Yea. That's also a point. And you can make many more friends there."

"I don't think so. 'Cause this was my first ever first circle. I never had friends before except for Jane. Actually, I never made friends 'cause I knew it was useless. I knew that had to leave the place in a year or two. But, after I came here, I had a very unique and different experience. The girl, whose name was barely known by anyone in the entire session, became the most famous girl just in five minutes. The girl, who used to avoid interaction actually became someone's enemy, someone's friend, pretended to be someone's girlfriend, dared to break the school laws, passed the first test of the session by cheating, and became class representative. The things which I never did in my entire sixteen years, was all done by me in just two months."

Ava looked at me with a soft smile and asked, "So, you don't wanna leave the school, right?"

"No, I don't wanna leave."

"But still you're leaving..." her eyes were filled with tears though she was strong enough to control her emotions so she didn't cry.

"Sorry Ava, I can't hurt my father because of anyone."

She relaxed by closing her eyes and taking her tears back in her eyes.

Then said, "It's okay. I can understand. After all, parents are the most important thing in the world."

I hugged her and said in a soft tone, "Thank you, Ava, for understanding me."

She pushed me with a hit on my shoulder and said, "C'mon. Now no more emotional drama. We have these three-four days, let's enjoy them to create beautiful memories."

A smile arose on both of our faces and we went out to have dinner.

We came back late and tired as well, so we slept right after changing into the nightdress.

17
The Transfer

Alarm rang. I woke up rubbing my eyes. Ava, who was sleeping next to me also woke up wishing me morning. We got up with a smile and then got ready for school, ate the breakfast which was milk and bread and then we headed off to school. Ava insisted on driving, so, I let her drive the car and sat on the passenger seat.
While driving, she broke the silence and said, "Umm... Amelia, you wanna tell about your transfer to Steven?"
"I-I don't know."
"Think over it okay."
"Yep."

Soon we reached the school. Ava parked the car and we got down carrying our bags.
As we went to the class, Ava told Mia and Jane about this.
Jane came to me with a long face and asked, "Is it..."
Before she could ask it all I replied, "Yes, it's true that I'm gonna leave soon."
Mia said, "But why so suddenly?"
I replied nothing but sighed.
Ava said, "Hey, you're making her upset. Just two days are left. Why are you making her upset instead of making her

happy and bidding a nice farewell?"
Mia's eyes enlightened as she said, "Yea. That will be great."
Jane said, "How about we talk about it in the lunch?"
I approved and then we went to our seats as the bell rang. Steven came and sat next to me with the same expressions as he always has in front of me.
I was wondering, what will be his reaction after hearing my transfer? At that time, I didn't know why I was worried about his thoughts, but yea, at that time, his thoughts did matter to me.

Soon after studying for three periods continuously, we went to have lunch. On the way to the cafeteria, Ava asked me, "Hey, I'm gonna tell Rason about you. Eden and Zeo have already known it. Do you want me to tell Steven?"
I shook my head and said, "No. Not right now. I'll let him know later."
She nodded and we walked to the cafeteria, while having lunch, Ava said to reason who was sitting opposite him, "Hey, come out for while. I need to tell you something."
He denied. But then Eden convinced him to go out with her. He finally agreed and went out.
Before Ava could say anything to him he said, "Hey, before you say it, I'm making it clear. I'm not at all interested in a girl like you so don't confess."
She frowned with irritation and hit his shoulder and said, "Excuse me Mr, I think you think very highly of yourself. I wanna clear to things. Firstly, I'm neither interested in you nor in any other guy. Secondly, I didn't come here for this lame thing. I came here to talk about something serious. Amelia is leaving school in two days."
He asked widening his eyes with this unpleasant surprise, "How come it's too sudden?"
"Even we didn't understand. But whatever, we need to hide

this from Steven."
"Why?"
" 'Cause Amelia wanna tell him by herself."
"Alright."
Then both of them came and had their lunch.
Jane said started the topic by saying, "Hey, let's go to the ball to have some fun."
Mia responded, "Yea. That will be great."
Zeo said, "Okay! So we'll plan it for the last period which is violin class. Today, sir is absent so we'll be free. We'll sit in a corner in the music dorm and will discuss it."
All of us nodded in agreement.

    The two periods passed by. The last period was of violin lesson. The whole class went to the music dorm and freely started doing whatever they wanted to.
All eight of us sat at one corner of that dorm.
Ava gave the first suggestion, "How about we go tomorrow. Tomorrow we also have a half-day. We'll first go to the mall and then amusement park, then the ball and then at last...."
Before Ava could complete, Steven interrupted and said, "I won't accompany y'all."
Though I wasn't talking I asked, "Why?"
He looked at me with rolling eyes and said, " 'Cause I don't wanna see you. Happy? Of course, you'll be. As I am the disturbing element of your life. I cause you trouble. You hate me a lot. Of course, you'll be happy."
I tried to explain, "Steven, it's not like that."
"I don't wanna hear your explanation. You're just a freaking moron. You know what, you're a pain in the butt."
I didn't know how and when I offended him again but that was outrageous.
I stood up with tears in my eyes and said, "Great! Then congrats Mr. Steven, because after tomorrow, you won't see

me again." Saying this, I walked away and went to the door side to have air and control my tears.

After I went away, Ava shouted at Steven, "Steven! Though no girl on this campus dares to say anything I won't be that girl anymore if you dare to hurt my friend. She just likes having fun with you that's why she often says that she hates you, you're just nothing but an irritating element. But that doesn't mean that she doesn't care. She tries to be friends with you but you always show him a cold face and chase her away. What the hell you want. Well, whatever you wanna do, it won't concern you anymore, 'cause she is leaving the school day after tomorrow and tomorrow is her last day. Her father would have already arrived at the home to start packing. After that, you can be alone and in peace. Now happy?" After yelling this much, she came to me on the door side, patted on my back, and said, "Don't care about that stupid. Be happy."

I gave a sweet smile and said, "Yea."

While I was still standing there, Steven passed from my side. He was going somewhere, don't know where.

Soon, the period was over. Everyone decided on the plan and told me that it's a surprise for me.

I knew that I can't make them split out the plan so I gave up.

We collected our stuff from the class and then went to the car. Ava again insisted on driving after looking at my condition. That day, Ava was also returning to her home.

We went to the door and saw the keys hanging on the door. I could already guess that my father had come.

I went inside with Ava.

But as we both stepped into my room, both of our feet froze on the door and our eyes widened with mouth opened.

Ava whispered in my ear, "Seems I'm at the wrong place at the wrong time. Do me a favor. Get my clothes with you tomorrow in school, I won't even mind t=if you take them with you to the States. But I gotta go now. I'll taxi. Bye-bye."

I was still in a freezing position but was cursing Ava to leave me like this in such a condition.

The view in front of me at that time wasn't a pleasant one.

18
The Fight

The view in front of me was just like a view that can be in front of people if WW-III starts. Exactly! A horrible view.
 Because it was my father and Steven standing in front of each other looking into each others' eyes.
I don't know if that time they even realized that I came to the house already. There was complete silence and it was making the environment scarier.
 Firstly, I wasn't able to understand, why the hell Steven came to my house. I tried to make sure that they knew my presence in the room and pretended to cough a little.
But no response. Seriously, dude! That's my house and I'm just neglected like air.
Then I said clearing my thought, "Dad! You're here." Can you believe it? Still no response.
 I made a jaded face 'cause I myself was feeling like air.
I again said, this time, a bit louder, "Dad!"
Then dad said, not to me but to Steven, "Son, are you sure?"
After hearing this, I was feeling as if I'm still his daughter.
Steven replied to dad, "Yes uncle. A hundred and one percent sure. I'll take the responsibility."
I didn't know what they were talking about but I was

surprised by the tone in which Steven was talking to my dad. He was so polite! Like, I hadn't heard his tone this polite ever.

Well, I left thinking about this and listened to their conversation.

Dad continued, "Alright son. Then, I'll count on you for this. But, I have only my daughter as my family. Take care of her." Hearing this, I couldn't resist myself anymore. I went and stood in between dad and Steven facing towards dad. I yelled, "Dad! Am I still your daughter? You're selling me to him! You think he's trustworthy?"

Then I looked at Steven, who was smirking at me. Really clever! Pretending to be innocent in front of my dad.

Dad said, "This girl! How can you say this? He has helped you so much. He went to the school with you to ensure your security."

Dad didn't know that I was the driver.

He continued, "He also sat with you to keep you comfortable."

'Dad, that was the teacher's arrangement.' was the thought going in my mind.

He continued, "He even carried you and applied pain removal spray to your ankle when it got sprained."

'C'mon dad. You'll kill him if you get to know he kissed me before applying it." was the thought going in my mind.

He continued, "Say if these are false."

"Dad! Are you my father or his?"

"Sweetie, it was you who was wrong this time. Don't blame your dad. All his actions show such good care and how responsible friend he is."

At that time, the only thing I wanted to say was, 'Actions he told you were right but intentions were totally a bully.' But I didn't split out a word as he was already proved innocent in front of my father.

I sighed and said, with a gloomy face, "Alright. Say what I need to do?"

A big smile arose on dad's face and asked me, "Do you wanna stay here?"

I looked at him with a stunning face and said in a soft tone, "Dad..."

"Oh c'mon. Just tell me, you wanna stay here?"

"I-I..."

"Ah! I understood. You want to. Alright then. You can stay here. But you'll live in an apartment from now on. That Steven will show you."

"Dad, are you really giving me permission to stay here?"

He nodded with a hum and smiled warmly. I couldn't help but hugged dad tightly with happiness.

Then suddenly smile faded from my face and I loosen the hug and looked at dad and said, "But Dad, what about you?"

"Don't worry sweetheart. I'll be staying with my one of the close friend and he's my colleague too. So, I won't feel lonely. And whenever I'll miss you I'll call you."

I hugged him again, "Dad! You're the best. Thanks, dad!"

"Baby girl, don't thank me. Thank your friend, Steven."

"Don't mention him. What can he do? *looking at steven* You're still standing here. Just go. I don't talk to strangers, nor I allow them to enter my house."

Before Steven could reply, dad hit my head lightly and said, "Amelia, how can you talk to him like that? After all, when I'll leave, after that he'll be the one taking care."

"What? he? You're leaving me here at his responsibility? The one who can't take care of himself will take care of me? Are you kidding me?"

"Amelia, stop it. If not for him, I would not have agreed to let you stay here. He's the one who came here and pursued me

let you stay here."
I looked at him surprisingly and whispered to myself, "He...?"
Meanwhile, he pretended to cough and looked away. Of course, it was obvious. 'Cause he would never accept the help he did.
I finally agreed.
Steven went away after bidding goodbye to my father but not even a bye for me. How mean was he, right?
I stayed with my dad for that day.

As I wasn't going with him, he decided to go earlier. He easily got the tickets of the next morning, but too early. 4:00 AM.
I talked a lot after a long time. We talked till 2:00 AM while I was helping him in packing his stuff.
Just two hours were left, we had a little rest for 1 hour then we called a cab as reaching the railway station would take him 45 mins. I insisted on sending him, but he denied saying that he will go by himself. Hence, I didn't force him.
Soon the cab arrived.
We went downstairs.
Dad hugged me and said, "See, when I'm not here, take care of yourself. Well, I'm relieved as long as Steven is there."
"Dad, why are you mentioning him again."
"Daughter, I don't understand what grudge you hold against him?"
"Dad, I think you should ask Steven instead that what grudge is he holding against me for two-three weeks." Saying this, I averted.
Dad looked at me with confusion and was about what I was talking about. But I realized this and said in a breath, "Ayya dad, let's drop this topic. You'll get late if you continue standing here."

He got in the cab. The cab started and I waved goodbye to my father and after he went away, I also went to my flat and then rested for a little while before getting up again to get ready for school.

But soon, the alarm rang at 6:00 AM. Well yea, because of that crackhead, I became habitual of waking up early.

I woke up and hurried to school. Well, my initial plan was to stay at home to complete my sleep but I forgot that those people didn't know that my plan of leaving was changed. Hence, I got ready and went to school.

As I reached the school and entered the class, Ava suddenly jumped from nowhere and said, "Surprise!"

I was amazed and frozen at that instant trying to understand what happened.

Mia also came to the door and said, "So, how was our surprise. We told you, you're gonna have a nice surprise."

I was totally confused with their words and then said, "What surprise?"

Jane who came with Mia, said, "C'mon, what can be a bigger surprise than you staying here."

My eyes widen. I thought I was supposed to give this surprise to them but things turned out different.

I said, "How you people know that I'm not going?"

Jane said with a notorious smirk, "All thanks to Steven."

I furrowed my eyebrows in confusion.

Mia said, "Actually when you argued with Steven at the cafeteria and then left the place, we explained to Steven everything. And god damn! At that time, his expressions were worth seeing. We all were upset when Steven suddenly said that he'll take responsibility for you to stay here. Then he told us that he was going to your house to talk to your father and then went away."

At that point of instant, I understood why Steven was in

hurry.
After hearing this I was both happy as well as confused. I was happy from inside that he helped me but at the same time, I was confused that why did he help me.

I was determined to ask him.

Soon the bell rang, we sat on our seats.

Steven also came soon. It was the first time I was so happy to see him.

He came and sat down. I said with a polite voice, "Hey, thanks for your help yesterday, if not for you I..."

He interrupted, "Please, don't misunderstand. I didn't do it for you. I was afraid that if you'll go, then that Dona will sit with me."

"Tch! too proud to accept," I murmured.

The class started and we started studying. In the recess, we went to the cafeteria. There we started discussing a hangout.

Eden said, "How about we go to the amusement park today?"

Steven yelled, "NO! Today is Saturday."

Rason, "Oh yea, that means we can't go."

I tried to understand the situation and then said, "Oh c'mon. This is a modern world. You still believe in superstitions?"

Zeo, "Oh no-no. You got him wrong. Actually, he has some personal work to do."

I replied with a sigh, "Alright. No problem. Anyways, I also can't come."

Mia asked with confusion, "Why?"

I shyly replied, "My... prince will come live today."

Steven asked with dark eyes, "Your prince!"

"Yea... My prince. The Secret Pheonix. The best online singer. I'm his hardcore fan. But I never got a chance to meet him. Neither he do many concerts."

Steven smirked and said, "You think he'll meet a moron."
I replied with a rude voice, "Yea! He will. If he doesn't judge a person by looks. Like you. Jerk!"
He again smirked and said, "That's not my problem."
I averted here and there to show an intentional ignorance. But how can I expect any reaction from him? Of course, he ignored me even in a worse way and start eating lunch.
Jane whispered in my ears, "I think, you both should be locked in a room and you should take out your enmity there just at once."

I furrowed at her indicating to drop the topic and eat the lunch. We ate lunch and then went to the class. Meanwhile, I was thinking all the time that what this Steven do every Saturday. He has always been mysterious.
Next, I decided to follow him after school. I left at the same time as he left. I followed him with the car. He stopped the car somewhere and I stopped too at a certain distance. He got outta the car and started walking. I decided to follow him on foot. As I got outta the car and looked ahead, I found that he wasn't there anymore. Before I could guess where he could have gone, my mouth was covered by the palm of a hand.
But the poor guy didn't know that I was a black belt in Karate. I held his arm and tried twisting it, but instead of letting me outta his grip, his grip tightened more. I heard a familiar voice saying, "Better not try these on me. If you are the black belt at Karate, I'm the national champion of the same."
My eyes widened as I realized that it was the voice of Steven. He loosened his grip. I turned to him bending my head down to avoid eye contact with him at such a moment.
He chuckled sarcastically and said, "So, following me, huh?"
I knew I was dead but then too I tried to save my face

and said, "Who is following you? You think too much. Why would I follow?"
"How would I know? You need to tell me why are you following me."
"I'm not following you. I was just..."
He banged his hands on my car and now I was between his arms.
He said with cold eyes, "Dare not to make any lame excuse. Until now, no one ever dared to suspect me, who are you to do so?"
The way he was saying was embarrassing me too much.
I had tears in my eyes, 'cause I don't why but I was somewhere hurt by his words.

I said in a low tone but a rude one, "So for you I'm just a passerby. According to you, you can come to my home, talk to my father and do as you wish but if I just wanna know something outta curiousity then I'm wrong. He said nothing, held my hand, made me sit in my car in the passenger seat, and started driving my car. "Hey, how dare you? This is my car."
He ignored my words and kept driving. We reached my home. He took me inside, closed the door, and said, "Now say, what is your problem girl. Why are you just everywhere on the places you shouldn't be."
"You are no one to tell me who I am." I rolled my eyes and went to my room to bring my MP3 player to hear some songs to calm down.
He shouted from behind, "Are you even listening to me?"
I stopped and turned around. I tried to calm myself and then said, "See, I'm really sorry for today. I should not have followed you. Happy. Now please get outta my house and lemme have a rest."

Then I went into my room and turned on my MP3 player hoping that he will get out soon. I wasn't able to understand that why was he acting like this. "Did he not want me to be mad at him? No how can it be possible? He won't even care a Lil about me."

Suddenly I heard a door bang. Steven came inside, picked up my MP3 player, and threw it on the floor with the force that it turned off.

I shouted in my loudest voice I could take out, "STEVEN!"

Tears were there in my eyes with anger and sadness.

I picked up the MP3 player, tried to start it but I wasn't able to.

By this time I could see on Steven's face that he was regretting his action but he was too proud to accept it.

He said in a calm way, "What's too bad to cry about this? Have it *money in hands* and buy a new one."

I looked at him with fierce expressions, "How cheap you are! You think everything can be bought with money! This was the last gift my Mumma gave me. Do you think you can repay it?"

His expression got more regretful, but I ignored his regret as I was boiled up with anger at that time.

He said while shuttering, "T-t-this... I-i... I didn't.. m-mean that."

I took my eyes off him and looked towards the wall and said, "Get out."

"What? Amelia, I really didn't...."

"I said, GET OUT!!!!"

After that, he didn't dare to say anything and went outta the house to give me space.

I was still mad, but after my crying session for more than two hours, I looked at my MP3, checked it, and realized that it can be repaired again.

As I have a good temper that's why I can't remain angry for much time. I decided to forgive him for this, as I knew he was already regretting it. Also, it was me this time who started it first.

I took out my phone and called Ava.

She picked up.

"Heyya my Amelia. Wassup!"

"Umm... Ava, I've got a problem. Actually, I was trying to do something outta curiosity which I shouldn't and I messed it up all."

"Why? What's wrong?"

Then I narrated the whole incident to Ava.

After hearing it all, she sighed and said, "Amelia, I wanna ask you that why you got angry with him?"

"Because he broke my last gift from my Mumma."

"No, not that time, I mean the time when you got outta the car. I mean, according to me, he was right at this, you must not have followed him. Because you can't invade anyone's privacy like this."

Her question put me in a confusion. She was right. Why I got mad at him at that time.

Then she continued, "My silly Amelia, can't you realize it. It's not anger. It's jealousy. You got jealous of the people who are around him with whom, he is close. You feared that he might treat you just as a common person, not a special one."

Actually, every word from her mouth was true, but I didn't know why would it happen so I said, "How can it be. Why would I care about him?"

"Oh My God!!! Amelia, do you I need to tell you this. It means that you are in love with him."

LOVE!

Hearing this word made my heart racing faster and faster. I calmed myself down and said, "Love? How can it be? This guy has always poked me. Always used to gimme works. How can I like such a cold."

"That's why love is special. It can be with anyone. It has so many questions on it but still is beautiful. It can be painful but has the strongest healing power too. If love was so easy to understand, many people would have been love couples easily."

19
Charles Riddle

We hung up the phone after talking for a bit more time.
Even after we hung up, the words of Ava were still going in my mind.
But, I just tried to ignore them.

The next day, I was all set to apologize to that guy 'cause I knew that I was wrong. But, I also expected an apology from his side. As he must not have broken my things.
As I reached the school, I waited for him patiently. Soon the other three entered but Steven wasn't with them.
They took their seats. I turned back and asked Rason, "Hey, where is your friend today? He isn't here?"
"Ah! Yea, he said, he has got some works to do so he'll be taking a day off."
"Oh... Okay!"

I turned around making a tsk sound. Then the bell rang, soon the teacher entered. I sat straight and concentrated on my studies.
As the periods went by, we had our recess in the fourth one. We went to our permanent location, the cafeteria.
There, Jane said, with sudden excitement, "Guys! Wanna have some fun eve today?"

Ava and Eden were the first ones to jump from their seats in excitement and said together, "Where?"

While I and Rason just cupped our cheeks sighed after looking at the kiddish behavior of both of them.

They looked at our expressions and then sat down again.

Mia and Zeo had a date so they weren't with us. Good for them, they were having happy committed life.

Oh well, then, Jane explained that her one of the friend was throwing a party at a pub that evening and has invited Jane and her friends that means us.

All of them agreed. Rason was forced by Eden to agree meanwhile I wasn't ready to agree because I needed to find Steven but I got no good reason to disagree.

Hence, after school, as I reached home, I threw my bag and rested on the couch for 15 minutes. Then I changed the dress into some comfortable ones.

I sighed with relief from tiredness and then suddenly fell asleep.

After a long time, I woke up. I looked at my wristwatch and it was six o'clock.

"DAMN!!" I screamed as I needed to reach there by 6:30 p.m. anyhow.

I quickly got off the couch, rushed to my cupboard, and took out a shirt and black jeans to wear.

I quickly washed my face, changed my clothes, did my hair, and then rushed to the location.

Luckily, I reached on time. I searched for those people when I found Jane there. I gave her a loud call, "Jane."

She looked here and there to trace the voice and I waved my hand to make her notice. As she looked at me, she came running to me and hugged me lightly. Then we took a seat on a sofa present there and waited for other people to arrive. Soon, all arrived. We started enjoying the party. We

had some soft drinks and snacks like French Fries.
We were enjoying the party. I was dancing with full enthusiasm to feel better and better from that incident of the previous day. But when I was having fun, a guy came to me and started dancing with me. He started the conversation, "Hey"
"Hii"
"I'm Charles, Charles Riddle, from Ravon High School. And you?"
"Oh, I'm Amelia Somerson from Heather....."
Before I could continue, a hand came on Charles's shoulder, Charles turned around to see. It was Rason. Charles gave a weird smirk to him and said, "Long time no see, Rason."
From this, I got to know that they knew each other but they didn't seem to have good relations.
Rason replied, "Thanks to Steven, that you were expelled and we didn't get to see you often."
Charles laughed sarcastically which was clearly showing that he was angry at his response. But wait, Steven! How come he is always involved in such things?
Before Charles would say anything, Rason said, "Stay away from her."
Charles smirked and said, "Oh she is your girlfriend."
"Mind your language bastard. He is Steven's girlfriend. Not mine. And if you want your every body part in a sound manner then stop being close to her. Amelia you too, stay away from him. Don't talk to random strangers like him."
I nodded with my rest of the body still freeze by the coldness I was feeling between them.
Charles laughed in an evil way and said, "What if I do this?"
He took off the rubber band from my hair, making my hair messy. Also, he slid his finger on my cheek.
I was just about to slap him when I heard a loud voice,

"Charles, you dare to touch my girl!"
It was Steven. He came near us and without even thinking he gave a punch on his nose making him fall down and all the people at the party stopped. He held his collar and made him stand up. He was yelling at him while I was just looking at him without any blink. I was still stunned at his words when he claimed me as his girl. I was actually doubting if he was drunk that he said something like that. Oh no, a drunken man would actually say the truth so it can't be. Maybe he was hit by something.

I was still lost in my thoughts when I felt a hand over my wrist. It was Steven. He grabbed my wrist and then took me outta the pub. He made me sit inside his car. He sat on the driver's seat, still looking mad at what happened. This made me chuckle a little.

He looked at me in an unbelievable manner and said, "How come a girl is so silly. What if he had done something wrong. He would actually have if Rason wasn't there. How stupid you are."

He started looking out the window. I wanted to say it 'What can happen to me if you're there but I didn't say it. Suddenly, he heard him say softly, "Umm... I... I'm sorry. For yesterday."

My eyes widened. It was my first time seeing him apologize. Before I could say anything, he continued, looking at his hand which was resting on his laps, "I know I'm stubborn and short-tempered but I didn't mean to do that."

"It's okay. Actually, I'm also sorry for acting recklessly yesterday. It was me who followed you and tried to invade your privacy but still, I got mad at you."

"No, it's fine. Actually, I didn't know that your mother was no more. I just assumed it when I talked to your dad and he said you lived alone with your dad only by your side

but yesterday I realised that it's true. I can understand the feeling of losing a mother."
"Why? Your mom..."
"She was shot by my uncle's enemies. My uncle used to be a mafia. We cut all the relations with him because of that. Once my mom got a call that my uncle is highly injured and my mom was a doctor and it was her duty to serve the patient. There she was shot dead. She was..."
"Huh?"
"She was actually alive after being shot too. So, she was burnt alive, mercilessly. My uncle begged to let her go but they burnt her. They shoot the video of the scene and send it to us. The culprit Norman Riddle was caught and their whole gang was given the death sentence. But, his son, Charles is still here for taking revenge for his father's death sentence. My uncle was also dead because of being injured badly and not getting cured on the time. I still remember when I watched that video, my mom was screaming, she was running here and there with fire on her body to get help, but those people..."
There were tears in his eyes. He also tightened his fists as if he wanna punch them.
I kept my hand on his fist making him calm down. Finally, he did calm down in some time.

I also had experienced the loss of my mom, but not in this much pain. At least, I was able to see her dead body. I was all shocked to hear this. Who would have known that there was such a painful past hidden inside this ice face? I was damn disgusted by Charles and his father's actions. I was hoping that Steven doesn't get much upset. I started thinking of something to change this environment.
Suddenly I got a change in my environment when he said, "Oh by the way, here your MP3 Player. I've repaired it."

I was shocked. No, not because he repaired it. I know he is good enough to do it. But because, how the hell he got into my house to take it!

He knew this question in my mind. Hence, took out a key from his pocket and said, "Here, your father gave me this spare key before leaving."

I said with disbelief, "Am I really his daughter? How can he give keys to you?"

"Because he knows that kiddos need to be taken care of."

"Whom are calling kiddo huh?"

"You're smart enough to guess it."

"You..."

He chuckled at my angry face and then said, "Alright, wanna go home?"

"Hmm"

"I'll drop you."

"Okay."

He started driving the car. I looked out of the window to enjoy the scenery. Well, the scenery was just big buildings, malls and all. I was just looking out the window and was thinking 'It was the first time he was open with me. He has suffered a lot. No matter how cold he is, he is also a human after all.'

20
The Movie Night

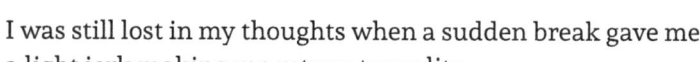

I was still lost in my thoughts when a sudden break gave me a light jerk making me return to reality.
"We have arrived"
Oh okay. It was already 8 o'clock. I was about to leave but didn't even open the car.
I looked at him and said, "What will you do now?"
"Maybe now I'll have some peace till I meet you tomorrow."
"tsk. So mean. I'll go then."
I was about to leave when he held my hand and said, "You wanted to ask something?"
"Umm... yea."
"Go ahead. I'm all my ears."
"Can you come to my house? I mean should we watch a horror movie? Today's plan was already ruined."
"Okay, but are you sure you can watch it?"
"You think I'm a coward?"
"I dare you not to flinch in the whole movie. Can you?"
"Bet?"
"Bet! but I'll choose the movie."
"Okay. Let's go!"
We entered our house. This was the first time when we

acted friendly in whole 4 months.

I changed the dress into a t-shirt and shorts. He was already in a comfortable T-shirt and pajamas.

When I came to the living room after changing, he already put the popcorns, pizza slices which he ordered when I don't know.

Then I came and sat beside him on the couch. He selected a movie from Netflix.

The movie started. Everything was going well. Suddenly there was all silence in the movie. The main lead got up from the bed to drink water. As soon as she reached the fridge before she could open it, I heard a loud shouting sound in my left ear and I flinched and jumped a little with a little scream, meanwhile, on the T.V. she just took out the bottle casually.

I looked at Steven with a death stare. He laughed and said, "You can even get scared from my shout. Haha."

"Stop laughing."

"Alright alright. I'll stop. But you lost the bet."

"Okay, alright. I lost. Happy?"

Then we both continued to watch it. After that, there were so many scenes where I flinched making him laugh every time I did so."

At nearly, 11 p.m. we completed the movie.

I sighed with relief, "Hash! Finally, it's completed."

Then I suddenly felt a heavyweight on my shoulder. It was his head. I realized that he was already asleep here. Also, he was holding my hand. The movie was so horrified that I didn't realize at the movie time when he slept and when he held my hand.

I had always felt hardness and toughness whenever he used to hold my hand for any of the reasons. But this time, it was different. His hands were just softly holding mine. 'He cares about me?' was the question that came to mind and made me smile softly. But the answer my mind gave to this vanished my smile, 'C'mon he is asleep, he can't keep his grip tight.'

I sighed and tried to let my hand get free from his grip. As I tried to take out my hand, his grip suddenly tightened and held my hand like a scared child and started murmuring something but loud enough that I was able to hear, "No... Mumma, don't go. They'll kill you. They'll burn you. Please don't go."

I patted his forehead to make him calm and asleep and making him reassure I was thereby saying, "Don't worry she won't go anywhere."

He soon became silent and slept. I dared not to stand from there as he was holding my hand tightly.

Luckily there was a blanket near you. I took the blanket with your free hand and started covering both of us when suddenly his head fell on my lap. I tried to move him from my lap but I was afraid that he would wake up. Hence, I covered both of us with a blanket and kept sitting as it was improper to sleep with a guy in such away. Well, I didn't realize when I also slept while sitting there.

   The next day, surprisingly, I woke up in my bed. How it happened I didn't have any idea.

I looked at the clock, it was 8 a.m. and I had calm expressions after I realized that it was Sunday.

I got up from my bed, did my hair, tidied my bed, and then went out into the living to check on the living room. But there was no one there. I smelled something nice from the kitchen and went there.

The food was kept there covered with a plate and note beside it.

> *"I'm sorry to sleep here last night. I woke at 1 a.m. yesterday and found you sleeping in uncomfortable so I just took you to your bedroom and let you sleep there. Then I went to the living room and slept on the couch. I woke up at 6:30 a.m. and then prepare this breakfast for you before leaving. Remember to eat it. Also don't need to worry about cleaning stuff. I've already cleaned your house.*
> *-Steven"*

I smiled at the letter and then uncovered the plate and found two sandwiches and four rice balls that he made himself.

I quickly ran to the bathroom, did all the morning domestic chores, and came to have my breakfast after getting ready.

As I tasted both the things, they were really delicious. I kept on smiling while eating my breakfast.

After I was done with my breakfast, I washed my plates and then quickly grabbed my phone.

I opened his text to say thank you.

I wrote: Thank you so much for today.

After texting this to him, I scrolled down to see our old chats.

We just have texts like, *Come here in 5 mins.* and I had *okay.*

We had a lot more like this only, where he used to order me and I either would say okay or will refuse by saying 'do it by yourself.'

I chuckled seeing those chats, suddenly I came back to reality and patted my face and said to myself, "Don't act like silly. You need to study. It's Sunday, the only free day you get to study."

Then I took out my books and copies and started studying.

My whole routine that day went like this. I studied, used my phone, cooked, ate, and then slept.

The next day, I went to school with full enthusiasm but my whole enthusiasm just went out like water when I heard people gossiping about Saturday's incident at the pub. I really don't understand are our lives so much interesting than theirs that they need to discuss us.

I ignored it and went to class. Suddenly Ava came and jumped in front of me and said, "Amelia, that Saturday eve was so perfect. We enjoyed that scene."

I averted my eyes murmuring, "What to do with others if your best friend is like this."

I took my seat looking at her with a stern face asking her to keep quiet. She did the same.

But how can I forget that trouble girl in our class?

Dona came to me with her usual angry face and said, "Amelia, you dared to seduce two people at a time you bitch!"

We people didn't even care what she was saying as 99.9% of her things were just useless.

I ignored her until she said, "I doubt if your mom was the same as you, bitch! Hovering over the other men."

Before I could look up to slap hard, she already got a slap on her face.

It was Steven who slapped her.

Then he said in a fierce voice, "Don't ever dare to take out those words again you bitch!"

"Steven, you're taking Amelia's side after what happened yesterday? You saw it yourself that she was hooking up with another guy."

"That doesn't matter to you what she was doing."

She looked at me in a disgusted manner and said, "You do have guts to seduce a man with such an ugly figure you slut."

This made my anger on the highest level. I couldn't help it anymore and shouted, "Watch your mouth you bitch. You should be luckier that Steven doesn't really hit girls so his hand went soft on you. If it was me, then I wouldn't have shown any mercy."

After saying this much, I just sat on my seat with Steven sitting beside me.

The teacher soon came to the class.

She opened her book and started teaching us.

In between the class, Ava patted on my shoulder. I looked behind and she whispered, "Wow Amelia. You were so cool that time. Not only you but also Steven. Like, how come he is always there at the right time? I think you should really consider him for being your boyfr..."

Before she could say it all, Rason hit her head with his pen.

"Ah" she screamed in a very low voice.

"What the hell do you want Rason."

"Stay silent and study and let others also study."

I also turned to the front side again and started studying.

As the lecture ended, the next lecture was free as the teacher was absent.

I took out the phone and opened the social media and went to the page of **The Secret Pheonix**.

I forgot to check out his new song. He always posted on one Saturday in 2 weeks. But as I went to the party on Saturday and on Sunday I had to study so I didn't hear his new song. As I opened his account the new song was posted on his page but not on Saturday. It was the first time he posted on days other than Saturday.

I turned to Ava and said, "Hey, Ava. Open your social media and take out the page of The Secret Pheonix."

"Yea, I opened it. But he has not posted this Saturday. How

can he do it."
"Ah! Just open his page. He has posted."
She quickly opened his page and widened her eyes with excitement and said, "He posted!"
"Yea, he did. But don't you find something suspicious?"
"What?"
"Just look at the at the day he posted."
"It's... SUNDAY??"
"Yea isn't it surprising."
Steven suddenly said, "Can't you see his description? He said he was busy on Saturday hence, he posted on Sunday."
I looked at the description and said, "Oh yea. He did write that. But wait, how do you know? You also listen to him?"
Hearing this, Steven sighed with a chuckle and said, "Have I gone mad to hear him. I just heard this from somewhere."
Ava smirked and said, "Since when you became a gossip guy and hear other people."
Rason sighed and said, "Ava, we have got ears and we can hear if anyone will say it loud. Everyone is not a gossip person like you."
Ava made an angry and cute expression and said, "Dare say that again."
Rason chuckled at her face and said, "Silly."
Ava was about to continue but I stopped her and said, "Hey, stop it. We need to guess what was he doing on Saturday?"
Steven said opening his water bottle, "Such a gossip girl."
I ignored him totally.
Ava said with bright eyes, "Could it be that he went on the date with his girlfriend, like movie watching."
As Ava said it, Steven started coughing hard with water still in his mouth. While Rason started laughing like he has got a nice scene to watch but we were confused that what happened to both of them.

I rubbed Steven's back and said, "Are you okay?"
He said nothing but just nodded. While Rason was still laughing. Ava was getting irritated as he was laughing and she didn't know the reason.
Being irritated by his laughter, Ava said, "Can you stop laughing? Just laughing without any reason. Huh."
Rason said teasing her, "I've my reason that I'm laughing. Why does it concern you?"
Ava replied, "Ugh! You suck."
Rason, the sharp-tongued guy said, "Then why to talk to me?"

Steven cut their talks by saying, "I have said thousands of times, flirt outside the classroom. Let me study."
Rason made a disgusted expression and said, "Good for you Steven. Took the revenge just at the point itself."
Both I and Ava were feeling dumbfounded as their single word wasn't making any sense to us as they were talking in a mysterious way.
How mysterious this guy was that their simple talks seemed to be so suspicious then he would say <u>don't invade my privacy</u>. How come such people exist.
Well, soon the recess started. We went to our place.
We started eating and asking about the date of Mia and Zeo. They really enjoyed their date. And just look at us who just created a scene in a pub nothing else.
"Seems you people didn't enjoy much," said Zeo teasingly.
"Says who?" said Steven.
I looked at him widening my eyes to ask in expressions as if he was talking about the previous night. He raised his eyebrows and smiled a little indicating 'yes'.
But at that time, Eden noticed me and Steven talking in expression and suddenly, "I know how Steven enjoyed his

day. He must be with Amelia the previous night after returning from the pub."

I was about to deny it but Steven said at the same time, "Wow Eden, how come you became at guessing."

Hearing this, except for Rason, everyone's eyes widened with surprise and all started looking at me. I dig my head in my arms which were resting on the table. I was feeling embarrassed.

Zeo smirked and said, "Yo... Steven I never knew you were this romantic."

Steven cleared his through and said, "I guess it wasn't me who gave this idea of staying at her home and watching a horror movie till 11:30."

Mia exclaimed, "Amelia said you... to stay with her?"

Jane continued, "To watch a movie..."

Rason added, "Also, to let him stay at her home for the whole night."

Ava laughed and then said, "As I remember someone used to say, how come such jerk exist. What does he think of himself, is he a celebrity that I need around me? I don't need him at all. If only I get the chance, I..."

Before she could continue, I turned my head up and said loudly, "Done. Ava, stop here."

Steven looked at me and said looking towards Ava, "Continue."

She was about to speak but before she could speak I cut her off and said, "Why she should. She's is just speaking nonsense."

Rason cut both of us off and said, "But why you did so Amelia?"

He was right. Why I did so?

I think I got the answer within a minute and the answer which was coming from my inner voice was that I LIKE

HIM. I REALLY STARTED LIKING STEVEN.
But I knew that I couldn't say it there and hence I said, "I did this to return the favor of him helping me out in the pub. Hence, I invited him to watch a movie with me. But when the movie ended he was already asleep so I let him sleep there only. Nothing else. Also, I slept in my bedroom and he slept in the living room."
But Steven instantly said, "But as I remember, at first I was sleeping on yo..."
I cut him off by saying, "Okay. Let's stop this here. You're saying as if you did nothing."
He replied innocently and being acting unknown, "Did I?"
I was thinking not to bring it up but now I needed a tit for tat.
I said smirking, "Someone called me his girl in the pub. I guess it was you, Steven"
By just this line he was all freezer. His all evil smile changed into a very funny ignorant expression and he replied, "M-my tongue slipped by chance."
I raised my eyebrows, smiled, and then said, "Oh really? It's okay maybe. But you also picked me in your arms and took me to my bedroom when I was asleep. Also yesterday's breakfast... you made for me before leaving."
"Girl, that is called expressing gratitude," he replied.
I looked at him but not with a happy face. I just left the place saying nothing to anyone.
I started walking in the corridor when Steven came to me, "What happened? Haha, you can't beat me in teasing." he smirked.
I averted and said, "Steven I hope you can differentiate between teasing and spilling out some secrets which must be between two people."
"Oh, c'mon didn't you also say anything."

"Steven, I wasn't about to but you made me do this. You just spilled everything as if after they get to know it all I can face them without embarrassment. I'm really disappointed Steven."

Steven's face showing that he was in regret. Anyways, he did not know how to get along with people as it was the first time he tried to get along with the whole group I guess. And also he looked really innocent when he was in this state. I gave up after I melted on how he was feeling bad.

I sighed, "Alright, don't do it again."

He looked at me and smiled just a little and said, "That's mah gurl."

saying this, he flicked my hair with his fingers and then ran from there to catch up with his three friends.

I chuckled and smiled softly and said in a low tone looking at his back which visible from far, "I think, I've really fallen for you, Steven."

21
I Fell for Him

I was still looking at him with a smiling face when I suddenly felt a hit on my back. No doubt that I realized in a second that it was Ava. No one would be that mischievous.
She looked at my face and then towards the directions where my eyes were until she came. She found Steven and his group, "What are you looking at, girl?"
I blinked my eyes fastly for 2 seconds and said, "Umm... I... nothing." and then faked a smile.
Ava sighed and said, "You both really treat us as fools. Well, whatever. Hey, did you notice that he's changing into a soft guy? Of course, for us, he is still the same but he is being soft towards you. Sometimes, I notice that he smiles towards you but then when you look at him, he makes a rigid face. How proud he is to accept that."
"Ava... Ava... don't talk so much nonsense. People change with time."
"Oh really? Then my dear explain this, why someone changes with only one person? Why is he still the same for others? You know even when you went away from the cafeteria, he told us not to tease you by any of this 'cause he was just having fun with you. And also, he said it all

with that cold and rigid face and cold voice. My dear, people sometimes change because of love."

I really wished to believe her but by this, I would just keep some expectations that are impossible.

I just hit her head softly with my hands and commanded her to walk to the classroom for the next class.

She did as I said and we both headed to the classroom.

As I had realized how I felt for him, I was then feeling nervous to sit beside him. A thought ran in my mind, 'C'mon Amelia, how can you be so stupid. You usually sit with him. Can this love make you silly? No way. It can't be.' I was still fighting with my own mind when Steven's voice hit my ears saying, "You wanna stand like this till the school got over?"

"Ah, no-no. I was just having fresh air."

"I guess we get fresh air in the corridor which is all open from one side, not in the class which is closed with 4 walls."

One more thought went across my mind, 'This guy. He can really make someone speechless on his questions'

Still, I smiled, and said, "Oh sorry, hehe I forgot."

I sat and he chuckled saying, "Weird people exist"

I replied, "Who can be weirder than you here?"

"The one sitting beside me."

"Steven, you really have got the ability to piss off the people the worst."

"That's called talent."

"Argh... I lose. Now shut that stupid mouth of yours. No one can debate you."

Suddenly, a loud voice made me flinch and sit straight. It was our literature teacher.

We wished her good morning and then sat down silently.

She said, "Students, I've got a good piece of news for you. Your summer vacations are starting from the upcoming Sunday."

All the students started smiling brightly except for me because this was the time I hated the most. I had no one to spend time with. Also, my father was in a different country, so, I couldn't trouble him. I made a long face. Suddenly Ava said, "Hey, Amelia, this time my mom will go on a trip in my vacations with her friend. I don't wanna go there. Can I stay with you on vacation?"

My face brightened up and I exclaimed, "Sure Ava! You can. Actually, I was already thinking about how to spend these vacations alone. If you'll be there then I'll feel better and will enjoy my vacations."

Ava got even more excited than me and said, "That's great! Now I don't have to go on that boring vacation anymore. I'll ask my mom about this today. I'm sure she'll agree."

Not only us, but all the people also started talking about the vacations except for my and Ava's bench mate. Such boring guys were really sitting near me. They were still studying the stuff they want to.

"How boring," said Ava looking at both of them.

Rason replied to Ava while still looking in the book, "It's okay, usually brainless people call us that. I can understand."

He really had a sharp tongue. Thank god, I didn't say a word.

Ava averted with a tsk sound as she really used her brain this time and avoided arguing with him further.

Suddenly, the teacher banged her table and said in loud voice, "Silent! Now there is one more announcement. You'll be having a debate competition. I need to have two names from our class. And you'll be competing with other schools. One name is already been decided. Steven. He's really really good at debating. Anyone else?"

I whispered to myself, "He indeed is best in this thing."

Jane raised her hand. The teacher asked, "Oh Jane, you can debate?"

Jane replied, "No ma'am not me. It's Amelia. In our previous school, she has won 4 awards in the debate competition."

I widened my eyes. I actually like to participate in these kinds of stuff but this time, it was Steven who was going to be my partner.

The teacher looked at me and said, "Okay, then it's done. Amelia, I'm finalizing your name. okay?"

I nodded with a sigh.

Then the teacher started teaching.

While I was thinking what if I get nervous in front of him at the time of the debate.

I kept thinking about it and after the period was over we both were taken by the teacher in her staff room.

She sat on her chair while we were standing in front of her quietly.

She took out a notebook to fill in our names, class, ages, and school name.

Then she said, "Okay, so we have the topic, "What is more important? Love or money? And the good news is whichever team chooses the topic first will be given the topic of their wish only. They have not replied yet. You wanna choose the topic?"

Steven said instantly, "Love. We will go for love."

My eyes widened that how come this ice face will actually be able to speak on this topic.

But the teacher nodded and moved towards me and said, "Amelia, you go for the same?"

I nodded. She took out her phone, called the hosting committee, and told them our topic. Luckily, we were the ones to tell them our opinion side hence, we were given love as the topic."

After talking to the committee, she hung up the phone and said, "Okay then, you may go to your classes and make sure that you prepare well."

We nodded and thanked her. Then we got outta staff room.

I sighed and looked towards Steven and said, "Are you sure you can speak on such a topic."

"See, we must always take advantage when we are given the privilege to choose first. A person who doesn't know love will go for money. Well, no person is there who has no love. If a person is given choice between his mother and money, he'll go for money, if a woman is given choice between a million-dollar and the man she loves, she'll choose her man. Hence, proved money cannot win over love."

Though he is cold like ice he actually knew the value of love over money in a way that I didn't think.

I looked at him and smiled while he was walking. He suddenly stopped walking and I stopped with him too in a confused manner. He looked at me and leaned towards me and said in a low voice, "Can you stop staring?"

I blinked my eyes and started taking large steps towards my class feeling embarrassed of what I was doing.

As we reached the class, the next teacher had already arrived. She allowed us in and we sat on our seat.

After the school day was over, I was set to go when Steven held my wrist to stop me and said, "So, when do we need to practice."

I remembered that we need to practice too.

Then he continued, "How about I pick you up today at 5 o'clock."

"Where will we go then?"

"Umm... I've my studio, sort of thing. It's very quiet and nice place. We can go there."

"Studio?"

"Yea, my mom gifted me. Actually, I... used to like singing a lot. So, she gave me that as a gift."
"Wow. I also wanna hear your sing."
"Since, my mom has gone, this Steven has stopped singing."
I couldn't say anything on that. I just nodded and said, "Okay, I'll be ready at 5 o'clock. Now I gotta go. Bye."
He nodded and I went away.
Finally, after reaching home, I quickly changed my clothes and then had nap for 30-40 mins.
After waking up, I opened my books to once go through what was taught.
After this I ate some snacks which were there in refrigerator. Till that, the time was already 4:30 p.m. so I changed my pajamas into jeans keeping the t-shirt same.
Sharp at 5 o'clock, Steven was there at my place. I must say that this guy is really punctual of time.
I went downstairs and sat in his car.
He started his car. We soon reached to his studio. It was a clean place. Not so big but at least open room.
He also had studio mic and the DJ. I was amazed by this. I really liked to sing but it wasn't the time to tell him this.
He placed my bag on the corner table. We both sat on a carpet.
We started preparing for the debate.

For continuously four days, we were having this schedule. We used to go there and practice for two hours. But those four days were golden days for me 'cause I saw his other side which was a bit childish one. He would pout in anger when I didn't listen to him and would just make fun of him in any of the way. I even saw his childhood photo in which he wore a frock. I swear I was laughing hard. I wanted to stop my laughing to not to make him feel more embarrassed but I wasn't able to control my laughter.

He tried to snatch the photo from my hand but I backed off my hand and he lost his balance and accidentally. My laugh stopped automatically as I started feeling nervous and my heart started beating faster and faster when he came closer to my ear and said, "Either give me or I have my own ways." I gulped hearing this and silently gave it to him.
"Now let's practice further." he said keeping the photo in his drawer.

Like this our four days went, but in these four days I got to know his those phases which I never saw in school even for a while. I never knew that a cold guy can be this much childish too.

Finally the day came when the competition was about to start. We were ready in participation room.
Soon our name was announced.
We went to the stage. We heard the cheering of people of our school for us. Then our opposition team entered. My eyes widened with surprise when I saw that our oppositions had Charles and one more guy whose name was Peter.
Steven hit his fingers on my finger causing me to look at him. As I looked at him, he blinked his eyes softly to reassure that everything will be fine. I smiled at him to indicate that I'm fine not to worry.
The debate started and we started stating our point first.

22
Debate

Steven: So, we took the topic the love because we think that love is the purest thing that we can find on this earth. Money can never replace love which is true.
Charles: So you wanna say that love can solve any problem?
Amelia: Maybe no, but it can give us the power to go through all the problems.
Peter: Miss Amelia, I wanna ask you. If you go to a restaurant then you had dinner and when the waiter asks you to pay then will you give him money or hugs and kisses?
Amelia: Mr. Peter you are joining job, occupation, and trade with the emotion which is least required at that time. And of course, I'll give him money 'cause it's his right to take the money from me. And love won't take away the rights. Instead, it'll give more rights.
Steven: Absolutely, love would never take you down.
Charles: Then, Mr. Steven, if you have a girlfriend and she wants you to take her to the mall, take her to eat in a luxury restaurant then what will you do if you don't have money?
Steven: I'll tell her that I don't have money.
Charles: And what if she gets angry and asks for a breakup because of it?

Steven: Then, she was never worthy of being my girlfriend. If she loved me then she would understand me and won't ask for the thing which I can't afford. Because love makes is from selfish to selfless.
Amelia: Exactly. And if you were given the choice to choose between your love and a million-dollar then what would you choose?
Peter: Of course, my love. But doesn't this question directly aims the life? We aren't talking about life.
Amelia: Says who. I think you must know that the topics given to us are the most important topics of our life. And this proves that you'll go for love over money.
Peter: But then, may I ask why you did not count my question of the waiter as a part of this theme.
Amelia: I didn't say that your question wasn't related to the topic but it was aiming at the rights and as I have already clear that love gives is freedom and rights. It doesn't take our rights away.
Charles: Okay then tell me, if you don't have any money, can you build a house? Without money, can you buy a bed on which you can sleep on? Without money can you buy the comfort and luxuries? Without money can you travel the world?
Steven: With money, you can build a house but not the home, you can buy the bed but not the sleep, you buy the comfort but not the care, you can buy the luxuries but not family and friendships, you can travel the world but can't travel the past for enjoying the moments you lost. Can you?

By this, Charles was left without a word. The sounds of claps were heard everywhere. I wasn't able to believe that Steven can actually understand and explain the love in such a deep manner.

We got the victory in the competition and among all the

teams that came there, we both were selected as the best speaker.

I was really happy. From the next day the summer vacations were starting hence, we decided to celebrate on the next day as well as the first day of vacation.

After this, we got a lot of appreciation from the teacher as well as the students of our school.

The school got over.

I went home.

As I reached home, I quickly changed my clothes and started watching T.V. without bothering to have snacks as I wasn't hungry.

Suddenly, the bell rang. The first thought that came to my mind was that it might be Steven. But then I hit the head with my hand said to myself, "Don't be silly. Why would he come here for you?"

Then I rushed to the door to see who was. As I opened the door, I heard "Heyya," revealing Ava.

She hugged me tightly with excitement. I also hugged her back. At least she was the one with whom I can spend the vacations.

I welcomed her inside with her two suitcases full of clothes, books, and some makeup accessories.

She came inside, put the suitcase in my room, then she sat on the couch. I also locked the door. Then, we both started watching T.V. and eating chips which she both from her home.

After watching for more than two hours, we finally got up and Ava made coffee while I started boiling the rice for that day's dinner.

Soon the coffee was made and the rice was kept for boiling when we sat on the chair of the dining table and started drinking coffee.

Suddenly, I heard the opening of the door, but I ignored it as I thought it might be from my neighbor next door or on the upper floor.

But I heard the voice of Steven. His voice was soon coming towards the kitchen only.

"Amelia, what the hell is wrong with your door? This has got junk. Tomorrow, I'll call a bla..."

He paused and looked in surprise at Ava, while Ava did the same. My expressions were tensed one.

Ava exclaimed, "You!"

Steven also exclaimed, "You! What are you doing here?"

"It should be me who ask you this. I had already planned to live with Amelia this vacation."

He became quiet. Both of them looked at me, but one with a suspicious manner and the other with a pleading manner as if asking for help to handle this thing.

I looked at Ava and before I could say anything, she said, "What's going on here Amelia?"

Then, I made her calm down, made her sit on the chair, and explained to her that my dad gave him these keys. It was good that she understood the whole problem as she knew the previous incidents well.

Then, listening to my whole explanation she said, "Okay, then, I see. But, what is he doing here today?"

How could I answer her when I didn't know it myself. Still, I made up the story and said, "I called him. I act..."

He cut me off by saying, "She actually wanted to go with me to my house because she needed to learn some dishes and my maid cooks really well, hence I gave her this idea. Then, I told her to get ready before I arrive but seems she forgot."

I made a fake smile and said, "Yea, something like that only."

Ava, "Alright, then go ahead."

Then, she came near me and whispered in my ear, "Don't

forget to spend a good time with him. All the best."
I nodded with a small smile and then, changed my clothes and went with him. When we once reached the car, I sat in the car with him, and then I said, "You could have at least called me. Now she might think that I'm..."
"I know she likes gossiping but she is reliable enough that she won't gossip these things with anyone else than her two more friends."
His words made the point. Then I was about to ask him why he came today but before I ask him, he already understood and said, "I came here to pick you up. Umm... today, we won. so, I was thinking of celebrating. I know that tomorrow we all will celebrate together but at least today we both can celebrate. Let's go to my studio."
I nodded with happiness. We went to his studio and there, he had cake, some balloons, and pizza, a burger, and french fries.
I said in amazement, "Wow! that's looking really great. You're really good at decoration too."
"Umm... actually, Amelia, it's... my birthday today."
I looked at him with surprise. I didn't know that it was his birthday.
I smiled warmly and said softly, "Happy Birthday Steven."
He did nothing but smiled and then said, "After my mom passed away, I never celebrated my birthday. When my mom was there, she used to prepare many things for me."
I had watery eyes but a smile on my face and I said, "Your mom will be happy when she'll see you from heaven celebrating your birthday."
Then I asked him to start cutting the cake.
He cut the cake and fed me the piece of cake with his hand. I tried to do the same but he didn't let me do it and said, "I don't like eating it."

"Just open your mouth. I'm not asking for your opinion."
He really obeyed me like a child to which I giggled and made him eat the cake. Then, we ate the food, we laughed by telling our funny incidents to each other. Like this only, we spent our whole evening and then it was 8 o'clock. I needed to go home. I asked him to drop me. He nodded and drove me home.
After dropping me, I went upstairs. I opened the door and saw Ava coming inside from the balcony.
I asked her, "What were you doing there?"
"Well, I went there to have fresh air but witnessed something else too."
"What?"
"When he dropped you, he didn't go away till you closed the main gate of the building and then started coming upstairs. How caring."
"Aish! Stop it. Oh yea, by the way, tomorrow we'll be going camping okay."
She jumped in excitement and said, "Wow! It'll be fun. That's really sweet of you Amelia."
"Alright, alright. Don't thank me. Thank Steven. He's the one who planned it."
"Woooo... how come that boring guy became so interesting."
"Ah! Nothing like that. It's just that we're gonna celebrate tomorrow so he said that there should be a good way to celebrate. Hence, asked me if camping for 5 days will be good."
"Good? It's the best! Thank your boyfriend from my side."
"He is not my boyfriend."
"Okay, okay. Your future boyfriend."
"Shut the fuck up. Now let's binge Netflix."
"Yea... Oh, by the way, Amelia, I forgot to give you a compliment. You spoke really good today."

"Thank you. I guess, he was the participant the previous year too."

"No, not the previous year. Though teachers know that he's good at the debate but he didn't participate in the debate for two years when Charles left school. Actually, Charles used to be his partner in the debate but some things came up among these two also Charles started involving in things like abusing a girl, fighting with other innocent guys, etc. Hence, once, Steven and Charles had a fight because Charles beat Zeo. Then, Charles was found guilty and was expelled. Thanks to his millionaire family that he got a place in another school. Also, Charles is years older than Steven and is one year senior to Steven."

"Oh, I didn't know it. Well, bygones are bygones why to even remember that."

"Exactly. Now let's watch something."

We sat down and started watching the movie we selected.

23
Camping

The very next day, we were excited to go on camping. I and Ava got ready as soon as we could. We got ready by 9 o'clock in the evening and then waited for them to come. We had already packed the bags and all the stuff we would want there.

At a quarter to 10, Steven arrived with his car. But Steven wasn't alone. Rason was there with him. They came upstairs. As Rason and Ava saw each other, they started making as weird faces as they could.

Then Rason said to Steven, "Who asked you to include animals with normal humans on camping."

Ava looked at me and said, "Why didn't you tell me a headache was coming?"

They both gave each other a death stare when I hit Ava's head with my hand asked her to hurry up. She nodded and took her luggage. Steven already took mine so I only had a backpack to carry. As Ava, started walking with her luggage, Rason stopped her, took her suitcase from her, and said, "In this way, you'll surely fall down making our making our camping ruined."

Then he took the suitcase downstairs. We both were still

there only. She did a tsk and said, "Still caring about camping only. How mean."

I giggled as they both looked really cute when fighting.

Then we hurried up downstairs after locking the door.

As we reached the car, Ava asked me to sit on the front seat with Steven but I denied explaining to her that it would be awkward if a girl casually sits like this with him when his best friend is there.

She made a pout towards me and went to Rason to say something. While Steven was putting luggage inside.

After this, Rason looked at me and said, "Amelia, I'll be driving the car and Ava likes sitting in the front seat so, why don't you and Steven sit together?"

Ava hit his hand saying, "I asked for the front seat."

Rason rolled his eyes saying, "Idiot, can't you run your brain a little? The backseat will have no barrier in between like, gear and all. Also, they'll have more privacy in the backseat than in the front one."

Steven said while putting the last bag, "Don't you think that you both are too loud to let us hear everything?"

They both made a fake smile and then Rason said, "Well, then I'll driving."

Ava continued his sentence, "And, I'll be sitting on the front seat."

They got seated according to them.

After that, I and Steven also sat comfortably.

Rason started the car and drove it to the resort which was located in front of a beach and on its other side, there was a forest open for adventurous activities. We did not have to give money as it was owned by Steven's father.

In one hour and forty minutes, we finally reached there. At the same time, one more car arrived in which Jane, Eden, Mia and Zeo were sitting.

They came out of the car as did we. We did not need to carry luggage as there were men allotted to do so.

But when we all saw each other, I was surprised that Eden and Jane were holding hands together.

I looked at them and said, "Eden, Jane, you people."

They understood what I wanted to ask. Eden answered, "Ah, that... we are officially dating now."

Ava widened her eyes and said, "Oh, my god when it happened?"

"Yesterday evening," said Jane shyly.

We all were really happy for them as Eden was trying hard to impress the campus beauty and finally he was able to do it.

Then we all went inside the resort and went to our allotted rooms.

The rooms were like one room of two people.

I and Ava shared the same room.

In the evening, we took essential things and headed off to the forest and valleys in a car for camping for the whole night.

A van was given to us to keep the tents and other things.

As we reached there, it was already 7 o'clock in the evening. Hence, we decided to have a barbeque. Jane and I were good at this, hence we started setting up the thing of barbeque while all others went to search for the things we would eat.

Soon, they all came and we started making food.

After it was made, we all ate it and started playing songs nearby.

We were all resting when I started looking at them. I realized that I saved the whole luck of my 16 years for this. I silently get up from there and went towards the open area to have fresh air when someone came from behind and said, "What are you doing here?"

I looked back as I already realize it was Steven. I smiled and said, "Having some air." Then I paused for a minute and said, "I'm really happy today. Before I met you, people, I didn't know what it feels like to have a friend circle, going to such beautiful spots with friends. Thanks to you people who made me realize it.

He back hugged me and said, "Don't worry. You'll stay happy, I'll make it sure 'cause I've promised your father to do so."

I really wanted to be like this in his arms but I could not do it as I didn't know what he thinks of me and according to me, he didn't like me. Maybe he was taking care of me as a... little sister. I wanted to cry after this but I didn't.

I just said, "Thanks." and then loosened his hands from my shoulders and went away.

We had some fun that time and then went to sleep. The next day we woke up. I went to the bathroom which was created for tourists only. I took a bath and wore a crop top and shorts.

Everyone else too woke up and get out of their tents and did the same.

After this, we all scattered around in the jungle to collect food. We had tracking devices so that we could trace each other so that we wouldn't get lost.

I went deeper and deeper. I finally realized that I was very much inside the forest hence, I put my hand inside my pocket to take out the tracker. My heart sank when I realized that I lost the tracking device. I started shouted for help when suddenly someone kept a handkerchief on my mouth. I used my karate skills and directly attacked the stomach of the person but my attack didn't work as I started feeling weak as if I'll faint at any time. By that, I became completely sure that the handkerchief contained

something. Maybe, chloroform. But no, chloroform takes nearly five minutes to work on a person. It might be something else like that.
I fainted.

24
I Like You

I started hearing some noises as I started gaining consciousness.

I opened my eyes and saw Charles there with six more guys. I shouted, "Charles! Why the hell did you bring me here?"

He looked at me and smirked and said, "Your boyfriend has really embarrassed me a lot. In the pub, in the school and where not. He really deserves to be punished. But that guy, he won't feel anything if I had kidnapped him. But now, he'll risk his life to save you."

"He'll never come. He won't get into your trap."

"Let's see, if the love wins or his selfishness. And as long as I know, love always wins over selfishness right? Then he'll surely come."

"But, he... he doesn't love me."

"C'mon girl, are you fooling yourself or me?"

Suddenly, Charles got a call. He picked up the call, talked to the person for five minutes, and then said to one of those six guys, "Take care of her here. I'll be back in an hour."

The guy nodded and Charles went away.

I sighed as I was in such a condition and those people might be worried about me.

I then thought of an idea. It was the time to brush up my acting skills "Aish, bro, can you untie me for a while? I'm really feeling unwell. You just untie me for a second let me adjust to my position and then you can tie me. Also, I believe that if strong people like you are there then how can I even run from this place. Also, the gates seemed to close."

After hearing this, I could feel that they were feeling proud of themselves. But as they needed to show their reputation as criminals, they tried to be rude and said, "Okay, okay. We're doing it. But don't try to over-smart or else you'll bear the consequences. I nodded in innocence.

They really thought I was scared of them? My foot! Who'll be scared of these idiots.

Soon one of the guys untied me. But as soon as he untied me, I lift my one leg and punched that guy.

Before other guys could process what happened, I spoke out, "You guys really are so stupid. You actually believe that a girl who is kidnapped will not try to run. Such fools."

They all attacked me at the same time, but I was a karate black belt. They really thought of me as an easy girl.

I defended their attacks and attacked them back but slowly I started losing my energy as it had been more than 15 hours since I had something to eat. Neither I had drunk the water. The hunger and thirst were taking up my energy slowly. The five guys were already done by fighting. They weren't in a position to fight anymore. But till the last one, I lost my nearly whole energy. He punched me hard on my stomach which made me scream loudly and I fell down. Suddenly I heard the door opening with a loud bang. It was Steven and the police. Steven came in front of me and looked at me in worried expressions. While I smiled and whispered in a very soft tone, "You really came."

He looked at my bruises and then looked at the sixth guy

left. He ran towards him and started beating him until the police stopped him.
The six guys were taken away by the police.
Steven came running to me. He knelt on the floor and made my headrest on his lap.
There were tears in his eyes. I looked at him, smiled, and fainted.

I woke up in the resort room feeling pain on my stomach which had a large bruise and a bit of pain from the small bruises of arms.
I woke up and found Adrien sitting on the chair next to the bed I was sleeping and his head was resting on the edge of the bed and his hand holding mine. I smiled at him caressing his hair.
He suddenly woke up giving me the intubation that he wasn't asleep. As he saw me smiling at him. He held my neck and pulled me towards him and hugged me tightly. Then he loosened his hug and looked at me. I could see the fear in his eyes. It was the first time when I saw fear in his eyes. He again hugged me and said in a voice which showed that he was frightened, "You are really stupid. Couldn't you wait for me to come? Why did you pick a fight with them?"
I said with tears in my eyes, "I thought you'd not come."
"How can you even think like that? You know how much scared I was?"
I couldn't think of anything else but just to confess my feelings to him.
    I gathered my courage and said, "***I Like You.***"
His arms loosened. He looked at me with surprise and disbelief.
I again said, "I like you, Steven. I like you very much. I love you. I don't know how you feel about me but I lov..." he

suddenly pulled me with one hand on my neck and the other on my waist.

I was cut off by his sudden kiss. He kissed me. I didn't back off and kissed him again putting my hands around his neck. The kiss was very deep and passionate.

He was not stopping but kissing me continuously as if there was no tomorrow.

He finally pulled out a kiss after two minutes, looked into my eyes, and said, "I like you too, my Lia."

I hugged him tightly hearing this. He even kept a nickname for me- Lia.

The other six saw us from the gate and started screaming our names.

We suddenly loosened our hug and looked at them with surprise. Both Steven and me were shy.

Ava smirked and said, "So my little Amelia has finally got some brain and confessed. But wait someone used to say, who can like a cold icy guy like him. What? You changed your mind?"

I gave a death stare at her but not a serious one.

Eden said teasingly, "So, finally. This cold guy got someone who can calm him down and take care of him. Our duty of taking care of him is finished here."

We all laughed and giggled.

25

4 Months Later...

I and Steven are now a happy couple. He gets jealous whenever I talk to other guy but try not to stop me as he wanna give me full freedom.

Charles was arrested by the police.

Dona now no more bother us as she got her Mr. Right, Peter, yea the one from that debate competition.

Now I and Dona are on good terms.

Eden and Jane are also having a happy life. Same with Mia and Zeo.

Rason and Ava are still the same. But as we can see, Rason cares about Ava. Sooner or later, they can be a couple.

It is my birthday today. Everyone is celebrating my birthday at my home. My father visited me a week ago.

The time is 8 o'clock and the celebration is done. All started watching a movie while Steven asked me to go out with him for some reason.

He took me to his studio.

"Why did you bring me here Steve?"

"Actually, Lia I want to tell you a secret. I... I... am."

He caught the breath and said in a breathe, "I'm The Secret Pheonix"

"What!" I exclaimed in surprise.
"Yea, I wanted a nice time to tell hence, I told you today. I really didn't mean to hide this fr..."
I kissed his lips before he could speak further.
I said in a soft voice, "It's okay. I trust you."
He smiled and kissed me again.
Then he pulled out the kiss and hugged me caressing my hair. He said, "Lia, you're the best thing ever happened in my life. You're my first, my last, and my only love of this life."
"You too... Steve."

Then we again went to the house.
The movie ended and we all had fun after the movie. We were laughing happily with love, care, and joy in our eyes. Perhaps this was one of the best endings I could get.
I only had one wish to let Steven, **STAY WITH ME** *forever.*

> "*Guys, thank you so much for reading this novel. This might not be one of the best novels but for me it was first and the best novel.*
>
> *We always dream of having the best ending. But someone told me that best ending doesn't always means a happy ending. Sometimes, some phases are ended in the most painful way 'cause the next phase is going to be most beautiful one.*
>
> *It was a soft story wich might not have much of the twists and plots but I tried my best to make it beautiful.*
>
> *Also this is not just the end. Their college life is still left. Story of Rason and Ava is still incomplete which will be there in next part.*
>
> *I can't say when the next part will be released but I'll*

try my best to release it as soon as possible. Thank you."

The Birthday List Of Characters

- **Amelia Somerson: 5th August**

- **Steven Young: 8th April**

- *Rason Maxwell: 1st September*

- *Ava Collins: 19th October*

- *Janice (Jane): 6th May*

- *Eden Foster: 27 November*

- *Zeo Oliver: 16th November*

- *Mia (Michelle): 1st July*

- *Dona Maxwell: 23rd May*

-

THE BIRTHDAY LIST OF CHARACTERS

- *Peter Horan: 16th December*

- *Charles Riddle: 16th February*

- *Luna Adair (to be one of the characters in the next part): 22nd November*

Thank you so much for your support y'all. Stay tuned for part two.

CPSIA information can be obtained
at www.ICGtesting.com
Printed in the USA
LVHW022034120422
716030LV00005B/228